GOD'S
Hole-in-One
and
Other Miracles

D1603424

John W. Corfield

ISBN 978-1-64300-643-7 (Paperback)
ISBN 978-1-64300-644-4 (Digital)

Covenant Books, Inc.
11661 Hwy 707
Murrells Inlet, SC 29576
www.covenantbooks.com

I dedicate *God's Hole-in-One and Other Miracles* to my friend Gary, who challenged God to give me a hole-in-one. I'm forever grateful to him for doing it. I also dedicate it to these important people in my life:

My wife, Sherri. The Lord used her in two of the miracles, the Emboli Attack and the New Car Miracle. Sherri has an evangelist's heart and helped to rekindle mine several years ago. Without her encouragement, I may not have written GHIO. I am indebted to the Lord for giving her to me for His purposes. I couldn't have a better wife, grandma to our wonderful grandchildren, and friend on earth.

Two of my adult children, Troy Corfield and Tracee Swift, who prayed for me to quit smoking and drinking when they were six and seven years old. To them I am eternally grateful. I am also grateful to them for giving me four wonderful grandchildren, all Christians, and two great grandchildren.

My deceased wife, Donna, who always encouraged me in my ministry to Christian day schools and in my earlier evangelistic efforts.

Contents

Foreword...7

Preface..9

Part I: God's Hole-in-One

1   His Ways Are Not Our Ways.................................13
2   All Things Are Possible.....................................17
3   "You Can Definitely Count Me In!"......................19
4   "I Don't Believe What I Just Saw!" 21

Part II: Other Miracles

5   The Miraculous Healing of a Friend...................29
6   Sorry, Wrong Person; Right Number!.................33
7   The Chronicles of Narnia Play 36
8   The Christmas Play...40
9   The "Inside the Inn" Play Miracles 45
10   Flashback: The Straitjacket.............................53
11   That Night at the Jail 57
12   God Calling! 62
13   "It's a God Story, Son"..................................65
14   My Lifesaving Surprise 68
15   My Wake-Up Call 73
16   Difficult Times...77
17   Saying Goodbye 80
18   In Transition..84
19   My Gift from God 86
20   Love Thy Neighbor 89

21 Three Road Lifesavers 91
22 Our Miracle Car 95
23 "Lord, Is It Time to Come Home?" 97
24 The Presidential Honor Guard 109
25 Gary's Request..116
26 The 1776 Drill Team...118
27 The Divine Accident 123
28 "In Jesus's Name," Miracles...126
29 Time to Go On to Next Town...130
30 Impressions 132

Part III: Miracles of Others

31 Introduction to the Miracles of Others.................................137
32 Bob's Miracle..142
33 You Rang, Lord?..144
34 Bill's Two Miracles..146

Part IV: John Corfield's Personal Testimony of Faith in Christ

35 Faith Comes by Hearing...153
36 Sealing the Deal 163
37 My Wonderful Surprise 169
38 Making Beauty from Ashes...173
39 Grace upon Grace 178
40 My Cup Runneth Over 181
41 The Shema 187
42 The Biggest Decision One Could Make 191

Acknowledgments 195

Foreword

God's Hole-in-One is a fresh reminder of an essential truth. Those who are God's children have the great privilege of following His leading, instead of constantly trying to forge their own way through life. In the process they—like John Corfield—will experience miracles in their own lives that serve as reminders that their loving Father knows and cares about them.

Reading John's book brought back many wonderful memories of our ministries together: the joy of sharing the plan of salvation with so many during *the Jesus People movement*; of starting a church in a growing area; of worshiping together in spirit and in truth; and experiencing spiritual growth and blessing in both our corporate and individual lives.

I remember telling someone in those days that while some people in the church are like hands or feet or mouths in the Body of Christ, John is an "enzyme" in our church body. He encouraged everyone with his enthusiasm, which brought out our best qualities. With this book, he continues to do the same thing for those who read it.

This is a collection of fascinating stories of God's working miracles in the life of one Christian man from our own generation. It is full of Scripture quotations, theological truths, and apologetics. It is my prayer that it will be a powerful encouragement to many people and a catalyst for a great new awakening.

Pastor Ron Graff
Retired

Preface

The following is a story of an incredible event that happened over forty-three years ago during the summer of 1975. It is a story of faith, friendship, and an unexpected dare. It was so surprising that the following information must be understood before it is told.

In the spring of that year, the Lord Jesus Christ totally changed my life. In fact, I would say that the direction of my life did a complete one-eighty. Suffice it to say that once He had control of my life, He did some amazing things.

One of those things was the unusual, creative, and definitive way in which the Lord introduced himself to a friend of mine. In the process, the Lord gave me a second and very powerful confirmation of my new faith. It never occurred to me that this or anything else was needed; I was solidly on board. My conversion, which already took place several months before this event, was my first real and very much needed miracle. Nothing was going to change that. However, the Lord knows us better than we do. Although I didn't think another miracle was needed, apparently the Lord did. Whatever the reason, it was amazing.

Whether you're a Christian who enjoys golf or a golfer that has not yet met the Lord in a personal way, you will be amazed at what happened. Most golfers have prayed most of their lives for what I was **challenged** to receive. I know you will agree with the uniqueness of this story, but you may have trouble explaining it in any other way than what I have. It's not something that can be easily chalked up to coincidence. All I know is *it happened and it's time to share it.*

This is not my story—*it is the Lord's.*

Part I

God's Hole-in-One

CHAPTER 1

His Ways Are Not Our Ways

On a typical Southern California morning, sometime in the summer of 1975, my boss and good friend, Gary, asked me if I still played golf. This question would normally be unusual for Gary. From the time we met in early October of '74 to March of '75, we spent many weekends on the links. However, because of the changes in my life that spring, we hadn't played in months.

Prior to my finding faith in Christ, Gary and I liked to drink together, generally with his wife, and sometimes mine, on Friday nights. We would then play golf either Saturday or Sunday. However, this summer weekend was different. After my conversion, our usual weekend get-togethers discontinued. It had nothing to do with our friendship, but two other activities.

I had enrolled in a jazz piano class on Saturday mornings prior to receiving Christ as my Savior and Lord. Secondly, my main activity had everything to do with wanting to learn all about my faith. To do that meant serious Bible study. This was a conscious choice for the sake of my family's spiritual growth. Gary was and still is, in my mind, a good friend. Shutting him out was never intended, it just happened that way.

Therefore, when Gary invited me to play golf with him on that Saturday morning, I was quick to accept his invitation. Why he asked me to play never occurred to me, I was just happy to be his partner for golf. I hadn't played in a while and welcomed the chance to join him.

As usual, it was sunny but not too warm with a clear blue sky and light wind, a perfect day for golf. We liked to play at our favorite executive course, which had a combination of standard par fours and par threes. Later in the round, we came to one very long par three on the back nine.

As duffers then, this course seemed more forgiving. As for mulligans (repeating a shot to make it better), I doubt that we had any limit to repeat shots. It was fun to play golf together and this day seemed to be no different.

However, there were two exceptions, one minor and one major. The minor one had to do with my usual poor shots. Chasing a lot of balls out of bounds, *par for the course* (no pun intended) didn't happen as it usually did. In fact, I may have been playing my original ball the entire round. Besides that, for the most part, it was just another uneventful day of golf with a friend.

Uneventful, that is, until we reached the long par three. There was no warning that something quite unexpected was about to happen. Finding the right club to reach the green on the fly was always a problem for me. Hitting the ball well was usually the issue. Going from tee to green in one shot rarely happened. However, before making that choice, Gary surprised me with a very unusual request: "*Why don't you ask God for a hole-in-one?*"

That struck me as odd at first, but then I remembered my upbringing. As a Presbyterian, I had learned some verses of Scripture in Sunday school. They were mostly the Ten Commandments. We also learned the Great Commandment and the books of the Bible.

However, the verses I remembered mostly came from the morning Bible reading at our public school, something truly rare today. Those verses were the ones that stuck.

The reading was mostly from the King James Old Testament (OT). The main staple was the Psalms. There were some exceptions, usually before Christmas and Easter. Those readings came from the New Testament (NT) mixed with the (OT) Isaiah Messianic prophecies. They were used to explain the birth of Christ, His life, death and resurrection.

However, there were other exceptions. One principle, which I immediately shared with Gary, was we were not to *tempt the Lord our God."* (Deuteronomy 6:16, Matthew 4:7, and Luke 4:12 NKJV)

Gary laughed and said, "Come on! You've been telling me about a God that created the universe, the earth, and us. You also said God knew every individual by name before He did anything. If that's true, it should be *easy* for Him to give you a hole-in-one."

In a way, it was good to know he listened on our usual ride to work. In this case, however, I didn't know how to reply to his statement. Being a Christian doesn't mean that the Lord does everything we ask. We have direct access to Him 24/7, but our prayers are to be according to His will. Then again, could this be one of those rare moments when my nonsensical request would actually be His will? I rather doubted it, but there was only one way to find out; *pray first and hit the ball later.*

While thinking about it, I slowly walked onto the tee box. I carefully teed up my ball with the logo facing me. It was a *Top Flight* ball, but that was not the logo I wanted. It was the Bell Telephone Yellow Pages logo on the other side. I had inherited many of those golf balls from my dad after his passing. His clubs, which I purchased for him in the military as a Christmas present, were now mine. Those balls came with the bag, and most were new.

Dad had spent most of his career as a Yellow Pages executive for Bell Telephone in Pittsburgh. He liked to advertise the Yellow Pages to his golfing buddies. I did the same, but only because the balls were still in the bag. Being new, there was no need to replace them. Over time, most of those unique balls were lost to bad shots. At that moment, only two remained, which are still in my possession.

Like most golfers, I often prayed for good shots. And, as a new Christian, that definitely seemed like the best idea. However, that day, the motive of my prayer had to be different. Because of the unusual challenge, I felt it was more important to pray for Gary, which I did.

My prayer was something like: *Lord somehow let Gary know who the true God really is.* Believe it or not, that prayer was answered in a way that neither of us would ever forget. God proved to me once and for all that day—***His ways are clearly not ours.***

> *"Oh, the depth of the riches both of the wisdom and knowledge of God! How unsearchable are His judgments and His ways past finding out!"* (Romans 11:33 KJV)

CHAPTER 2

All Things Are Possible

Gary was the principal of a school in Southern California. I was a teacher looking for a job; which he provided. When I was hired, Gary and I quickly became friends. Neither of us came from California. We were both from the east, which helped us to get along well from the start. It also helped us to really enjoy our time on the links.

At this point, it's important to explain our spiritual conditions prior to my conversion. Gary had fallen away from his religion. He said that if he ever did become religious again, he would go back to the same denomination. I, on the other hand, made no such promise of returning to mine, which I never did. My belief is based only in Jesus Christ and His Word above all. Jesus is the one who saved us at the cross. It was not a church denomination or nondenomination.

Because of my relationship with Christ, on the tee that day, things were totally different. Praying for a hole-in-one with the express purpose of reaching a friend for Christ was a whole new mindset for me. It was totally out of character for who I'd been, as Gary knew me. Probably for that reason, my prayer was never confessed to Gary. I had prayed hoping he would receive the Lord and find the joy given to me.

Something had happened early in my youth that made me timid about that. A friend and I stole something from another friend. Afterward, I began thinking about God and felt that He wanted us to take it back. We gave it back and confessed that we had taken it.

However, when I said, God told us to give it back to you, he began to laugh. We even joined in with him. No one likes to be laughed at; we were no different. Perhaps that still influenced my decision not to say anything to Gary about praying for him. Whatever the reason, I didn't mention it.

My intention was much more than a hole-in-one. If Gary needed to know Christ as his personal Savior and Lord, I hoped a hole-in-one would grab his heart. Of course, that was out of my control, as it always is. The believer is only to obey the indwelling Holy Spirit. Therefore, we witness the love of Christ to others through His power, not ours.

The Apostle Paul said, "I planted, Apollos watered, but God gave the increase." (1 Corinthians 3:6 NKJV)

Winning someone to Christ is always up to God. And He does it His way and in His time, not ours. He may do it through us, but we never save anyone.

Looking upward, I prayed, "Lord, if it's in you to do this, I ask that it will be for Gary. And, if You do it, I will never tell anyone that it was my hole-in-one, I will always say, 'It was Yours.' After that, I took my practice swings and addressed the ball. A very important lesson in faith would be learned that day. A miracle really can happen.

"With men this is impossible, but with God all things are possible."
(Matthew 19:26 NKJV)

CHAPTER 3

"You Can Definitely Count Me In!"

On the tee that morning, it was hard to know what to think. My friend had dared to challenge God to grant me a hole-in-one. It's doubtful that he thought about it that way, but he really was daring our Creator for a miracle.

After sending the craziest prayer of my life heavenward, I took a deep breath and prepared to swing. Knowing it would take a great shot to reach the green, I decided to use a 3-wood. It seemed to be the only way to get it there. The fact that my wood shots off the tee generally had a little fade to the right didn't occur to me. This day was no exception.

I did hit the ball well, too well. It faded right and went way over the green. To make matters worse, it hit an asphalt cart path on the fly. Most golfers know what they would do next. They would tee up a second ball because of the cart path. The gigantic bounce forward would make it almost impossible to find without holding up the following foursome. Therefore, like any other golfer, I assumed that's what happened, and so did Gary.

In fact, he began to laugh, and to be completely honest, so did I. However, while I was reaching for another ball, his laughter was suddenly cut short. I looked over to where he had been standing, but he was no longer there. He was running full-speed, with his pull cart, toward the green. Had he seen something I hadn't seen? Apparently, he had!

For a second, I was really confused. The only thing to do was look toward the green and then upward. To my surprise, there was a ball, seemingly suspended, way above the green. How it got there is anyone's guess. I still don't know.

As it finally fell, it landed at the top of the pin's shadow. The ball began to roll toward the hole, as if guided by the shadow. It didn't seem to be in any hurry, which generally means it is about to stop. One would have sworn by its speed that it would stop about halfway there, but it didn't. Something special was happening! Would it actually reach the cup and drop? After all, hadn't I asked for the Lord's intervention?

As if walking, the ball continued to roll along the shadow's path to the hole. As I watched it roll and Gary running toward the green, I realized it was going to drop, and it did!

I don't know what Gary was thinking, but I, the believer, was totally stunned. My first thought was, *it may be someone else's errant shot*. What a coincidence that would have been! Quickly, however, that thought was erased. This had to be God's doing and the logo would prove it, which it did. Again, I looked to heaven, but this time to say, "Lord, I don't know if Gary will ever believe, but—*You can definitely count me in!*"

"Trust in the Lord with all thine heart; and lean not unto thine own understanding. In all thy ways acknowledge Him, and he shall direct thy Paths." (Proverbs 3:5–6 KJV)

CHAPTER 4

"I Don't Believe What I Just Saw!"

That day on the tee, I realized that John 3:16 was more than redemption. The Lord let this believer know that wondrous things will happen to those who believe in Jesus by faith alone. God's hole-in-one was a great one for me.

Before I moved toward the green, I was still trying to process what just happened. The best way to explain it is to quote the famed baseball announcer, Jack Buck, calling Kirk Gibson's home run in game one of the 1988 World Series: *I don't believe what I just saw!*

It was easy to understand what Mr. Buck meant that night. Gibson had a severe leg injury, but the Dodgers still activated him for the series. It was the ninth inning, and the Dodgers were down by two runs with two men on base. Tommy Lasorda, the great Dodger manager, asked Kirk if he thought he could get a hit. Kirk, hurt as he was, promised his manager just *one swing*.

As he emerged from the dugout, bat in hand, the Dodger fans began to cheer. There was still hope! However, as he hobbled toward the plate, their enthusiasm may have waned a little. Many wondered if he could even get to first base in the unlikely event that he would get a hit. That worry was soon forgotten as Kirk reached down to hit a low inside pitch into the right field pavilion to win the game.

As Kirk hobbled around the bases, the crowd went wild. The underdog Dodgers went on to win the series, never again needing the services of their injured hero. All true baseball fans, thirty and older, remember that one swing and what it did for an entire city and baseball as a whole.

During the 1960 World Series, we had that same feeling in Pittsburgh when Bill Mazeroski hit the winning walk-off homer to beat the Yankees. It was an event which had never been done before in World Series history. A walk-off home run to win the series has happened only once since.

To most baseball fans then, it was a given that no one beats the mighty Yankees. They were always the favorite to win the World Series. During a fourteen-year span, only three NL teams had pulled that off: the Dodgers, the Braves, and the Pirates. The other two were very good teams; the lowly Pirates were never even considered then to win the NL Pennant, let alone the World Series. We finished last or tied for last eight consecutive years from 1950–1957.

That series was really skewed in favor of the Yanks. They had scored fifty-six runs and the Bucs only twenty-five, less than half of what the Bronx Bombers did. And historically, the Yankees generally won game sevens. Yet, after letting them back in the game in the top of the ninth, we won with Mazeroski's home run in bottom of the ninth. It's known as the greatest World Series game ever.

The prevailing opinion among Pirate fans was it was a miracle, somewhat along the lines of the original movie, *Angels in the Outfield*. In the mid-1950s, the fictional movie about the Pirates winning the pennant with divine help was a big hit but hardly comforting. No one would have dared to think that we might win a World Series only three years later, and against the Yankees? No way!

However, while it may have been against the odds, the home run was not a miracle, at least not in the sense of the definition to be offered later. Maz had done instinctively what he knew to do; he put a good swing on the pitch. The result of that great winning moment brought Pirate fans and the city great joy, thirty-three years in the waiting.

I submit, as great as it was, it could logically be explained. Maz could even brag about it as the clutch hitter he was, although for the most part, that is not in his character. He still politely answers questions about it almost every day. It is said he still remains humble in his answers.

Whether or not his walk-off homerun was a miracle, *God's Hole-in-One* (GHIO) definitely was. To me, it was awe inspiring. I don't know what others may think, but for me, the Lord had answered my prayer in a miraculous way for Gary.

Gary knew I was trying to get the ace in the prescribed way, aim for the pin, and hope it drops in. Of course, that didn't happen. Thankfully, it was a more believable miracle because of the way it happened! But would God's message convince my friend?

Think of the absurdity of this event. No one would plan a hole-in-one as it happened that day. I didn't plan to hit it over the green, and especially not with the intention of hitting an asphalt cart path. That would have been absolute insanity, especially on this dare.

It would have been as if Maz had intentionally swung late to hit the ball to right field, hoping it would carom off something and deflect over the left field wall at the exact spot it actually did. Would anyone lay odds on that? Of course not, it's definitely absurd! That's the stuff of funny commercials, perhaps, but would never occur as a result of man's planning.

However, the hole-in-one did happen, and the way has to be considered just as absurd. Obviously, it wasn't my plan, but it was the Lord's all the way. Even if Gary hadn't challenged me to make a hole-in-one, it still would have been a miracle. But this one had to have a purpose other than making me feel good. It had to be done in an unusual and memorable way to get Gary's attention. I knew full well the improbability of accomplishing that feat. The odds are about one in twelve thousand, and that's by doing it the standard way.

A friend of mine saw a fellow golfer's drive change direction by caroming off a water pipe. It went straight to the green and dropped in the hole. That would be just as absurd as mine and definitely an oddity. However, mine was more complicated. God was challenged and therefore did the event His way.

First there was the dare, the prayer, and the errant shot. Second, golf balls don't generally bounce backward, unless they hit a tree, a wall, or a barrier of some type. Mine not only bounced backward, but upward so high in the air that it was hardly visible. I have never seen a golf ball that high in my life. To drop straight down onto the top of the pin's shadow and roll in from there is certainly against all odds, especially since it should have bounced forward, big time!

In proving to us that all things are possible with God, He demonstrated His great sense of humor. However, what's humor to one person may be frightening to another, even if they don't show it. Who likes to dare God and laugh about it, only to see the dare come true? Gary wasn't the only one laughing when he thought it wouldn't happen, I too laughed.

Whether or not this miracle was needed, I don't know, but God still did it. Obviously, the Lord had some other purpose in mind. Therefore, once it happened, I knew He had heard my prayer, which meant God had actually led me in that prayer for Gary. When we are in sync with trusting Him, he will direct our paths.

We know that all things work together for good to those who love God, to those who are the called according to His purpose. (Romans 8:28 NKJV).

When I reached the green, Gary was on his knees, staring down at the ball in the hole. The "Yellow Pages" logo was staring right back at him, erasing any doubt as to whether or not it was mine. Once I arrived, Gary flipped my ball to me and said, "I guess there's a golf god." I replied, "It is God, Gary, not a golf god." Obviously, he could hardly respond negatively to that.

It was overwhelming for both of us. Like Gibson's or Mazeroski's home run in baseball, an ace in golf is something any golfer could brag about forever. A lot of golfers spend a lifetime praying and trying for it, but more often than not, without success. However, after witnessing the unusual way this one played out, there is no way I could possibly take credit for it.

No honest golfer would ever brag about what happened that day. It could only have been done by God, which the Christian reader, golfer or not, will understand. As said earlier, His ways are not ours.

Today, I am still looking for that shot that flies straight at the pin and drops. The Lord would still get the credit, but at my age, unless He consents, it's rather unlikely.

Gary immediately told the starter that he had witnessed a hole-in-one. I appreciated that but was very relieved when the starter said, "Because we are only an executive course, we don't do anything special for a hole-in-one." Even if I wanted to, I wasn't wealthy enough to buy everyone a round drinks.

There are some things in life that are too much for coincidence. In fact, I happen to think now that nothing happens by coincidence. Therefore, it is and always will be God's Hole-in-O*ne*.

Did it really happen? Yes, it did! A miracle had definitely happened, *and both of us knew it*! But, at the time, I was still thinking—*I don't believe what I just saw!*

"Oh, that men would give thanks to the Lord for His goodness and for His wonderful works to the children of men!" (Psalms 107:15 NKJV)

Part II

Other Miracles

CHAPTER 5

The Miraculous Healing of a Friend

Eric Metaxas, in his book, <u>Miracles</u>, offered a simple definition from Webster's dictionary. It read: *An extraordinary event manifesting divine intervention in human affairs.* Although Mr. Metaxas didn't use that one, it definitely works for the miracles in God's Hole-in-One and Other Miracles.

All believers in Jesus Christ have or will experience personal miracles in their lives; it's a given, whether we realize it or not. Therefore, don't think of me as special in that regard. I will admit that my miracles may seem more numerous than most, but I am not the only one in that category.

Many think it's best to keep their miracles private. Others believe that God's workings in their lives were done to be shared to encourage others. Obviously, I am in the second category. Seeing how many were done in my life, it was obvious that I was to share them.

Also, do not read anything into them concerning me personally. I don't see myself as anything but a sinner saved by grace. I am not a miracle worker or a prophet and definitely not a healer. The Holy Spirit does all of that through those who are in Christ's body, *His church.*

He also works through medical professionals, such as surgeons. Some may have a relationship with Christ, some may not. The reader may ask, "How is that a miracle? A successful surgery can be explained through the natural laws determined by trial and error." That's true, but I am not referring to the surgeries themselves, it's the historical timing of the events. Here are the events to which I'm referring:

(1) The first successful surgery did not occur until the late 1800s, according to Jennifer Whitlock's article, May 6, 2016, *The Evolution of Surgery: A Historical Time Line* found on a website called verywell.com. That's approximately 130-140 years ago. My question is, Why did it take so long in human history to learn how to do a surgery?

(2) The article also stressed that most successful surgeries after the first one still resulted in death by infections until the 1900s. Why did it take so long to discover the cause and cure for many infections? Apparently, we didn't understand the influence of microbes in health issues.

The fact that God, more recently in man's history, released these secrets should humble us. A successful surgery and the cures for many infections are truly miracles, even if they can be explained. It's the discovery of them that is a miracle! Many more discoveries, which have occurred in less than one hundred years, seem to happen every day. With maybe five thousand years of human history happening after the flood, a hundred-year period is a very short time on any historical continuum. Why did God wait until the last days of the church age to allow them to be discovered?

These recent cures make unexplained healings throughout the centuries even more amazing, and they are still happening today. I witnessed a medical healing, which God brought about through me, in 1978. Although I have seen many healings brought about by God using others, I have witnessed only one which Jesus performed through me.

That experience involved an acquaintance, who afterward became a very good friend. He was hospitalized with Crohn's disease. At the time, I was teaching in a California elementary school. The patient, Ron, had told his wife, a colleague of mine, to ask me to visit him in the hospital. He was to have a colon resection the next day. When I walked into his room, I couldn't get over how pale he was. Apparently, he had experienced irritable or loose bowel for three consecutive weeks and, because of it, was scheduled to have the operation.

Actually, I was somewhat perplexed that he wanted to see me. I had briefly met him only once. His wife was religious, but never showed much interest in Bible-believing Christianity.

Yet, because of her husband's condition, she decided his request for my visit was a good idea. Perhaps she was hopeful that it would brighten his spirits and prepare him for his operation.

I also thought that it was a good idea. It was a good way to get to know him. While only a little over two years in my faith, I agreed to visit him. If my visit would make him feel better, fine, but that was totally up to the Lord.

Upon meeting with him, he let me know that we were brothers in Christ. That cleared up the mystery of why he wanted to talk with me. The meeting was very enjoyable after that. He shared his testimony of faith in Christ first and then I shared mine. All of a sudden, this visit had a reason, an exciting one, which only the Lord could fulfill.

Was it to help both of us grow in our faith? Yes, but there was a greater reason. It's always exciting to meet someone who trusts in Jesus. It's even more exciting when the Lord does something that can't be explained. He often uses a patient's grim situation to glorify Himself. It's also incredibly exciting when He uses an unlikely source to be a conduit for His miracle.

As our visit was coming to a close, I asked if I could pray for him. He said, "I was hoping you would." I placed my hand on his shoulder and began to say, "Heavenly Father, please guide the surgeon's hands . . ." What came out was, however, *be healed in the name of the Lord Jesus Christ.*

Where did that come from? I definitely hadn't thought it. Of course, it was familiar; I had read it in the New Testament. However, it never occurred to me to pray that. Even if I had thought of it, I wouldn't have said it. That just wasn't me, but yet, I said it.

It was like a dog hearing its bark for the first time. It startled me so much I jumped backward and immediately started to apologize. However, before getting out a word, he said, "Something has changed, get the doctor." At that point, I noticed that his facial color had returned to normal. When the nurse called the doctor, I wished him well and left.

All the way home, I kept wondering what had actually happened. Was it a miracle? Did I actually witness a healing? By the time

I walked in the door, my wife had the answer. She had just hung up the phone after talking with his wife. She had called to tell us that the doctors could no longer find anything wrong with him. All I could say was, Praise the Lord!

We were overjoyed. God had performed a miracle of healing, and He had used me as the vessel through which He did it. At that moment, the Lord's joy just effervesced in my wife and me. She had also been praying for his healing during the time of my visit.

But that wasn't the end of the story. The two of them, along with my wife and me, later attended Bill Gothard's Seminar, *The Institute in Basic Youth Conflicts.* It was a week-long seminar in Long Beach. That may sound like a teen ministry, but it was more for adults than youth. Ron and his wife both enjoyed it enough to want more. We decided to meet and revisit the Bible principles we'd learned at the conference.

We met weekly at their house until just before the end of the school year. It was the first time I had explained biblical principles to anyone by myself. I, too, learned a lot in the process. It was great for their spiritual growth and mine.

For me, it was enough to thank God profusely for using me in doing something wonderful. I was certain it would not return void. His Word never does.

Again, the credit is all The Lord's, as it should be. He allows us to have His joy, which is the greatest joy any person could have, but *the miracle or miracles always belong to Him!* My friend had been miraculously healed, and I witnessed it.

"And He healed them." (Matthew 21:14 NKJV)

CHAPTER 6

Sorry, Wrong Person; Right Number!

This miracle occurred in the fall of 1976. Later in this book, a similar story is presented, which concerned a distraught suicidal woman. By accidentally calling the wrong number, she reached a pastor. I experienced something similar, but it was the other way around. It was a somewhat embarrassing miracle during my first year at our California school close to home. My wife and I had become involved with the Campus Crusade for Christ *I Found It* campaign. Led by its president, Bill Bright, we were trained to do a two-week phone-a-thon. Its purpose was to explain salvation by grace through faith alone in God's Son, Jesus Christ. The motto was, "I found it—*new life in Christ.*"

Our calling headquarters were offices donated by local businesses. Each night, we were given a list of phone numbers. We had an opening spiel, and if anyone wanted to continue the call after that, we would ask and answer questions. I had some interesting conversations and occasionally had the opportunity to follow up with a face-to-face presentation of the gospel. However, the most interesting conversation was with a woman who kept interrupting me with questions about me rather than the Lord.

It was the last night of calling. I'd come to my last number, dialed it, and, once answered, I began this spiel: "I'm John Corfield from the '*I Found It*' campaign. That stands for 'I found new life in Christ.' We're calling people in the area to talk to them about their faith in Jesus Christ and . . ." The woman on the other end suddenly cut me off but didn't hang up. She said, "John Corfield?" Somewhat startled, I replied, "Yes." She said, "The teacher?" I began to tell her that I was a Sunday school teacher (remember, we are talking about God here), but she cut me off again. "I mean the school teacher. You're Kimmy's teacher."

At that moment, my voice went up about two octaves. "Is that you, Mrs. —— ?" She acknowledged that it was. I said, "I am supposed to be talking to a Mrs. Smith." She said, "I'm not Mrs. Smith, maybe you called the wrong number." I read the number back to her and it was definitely the right number but the wrong person. Apparently, that number had either been reactivated for her family or it was copied incorrectly by list compilers. Whatever the reason, I was on the phone with a mother of one of my students.

There were five hundred thousand telephones in that area back then; this was one I may have preferred not to get at first. What are the odds of calling a number, expecting to talk to a person unknown to me, only to find it was someone familiar with me? Since her daughter was a student of mine, the odds would increase to being more than one in five hundred thousand. The Lord really does work in strange ways. An argument can be made that it was definitely a divine appointment.

But it gets better. She was more than the mother of one of my students. She was also the wife of one of my college fraternity brothers whom I had never met. He was a principal of a school in another district. Again, the odds would be increased for that reason.

As I began to ask her about the people we knew from college, she cut me off again to ask, "What was it you called me about?" That gave me no choice but to relate my testimony to her. Feeling a little more comfortable, I said, "I'm a born-again Christian and part of the Campus Crusade for Christ '*I Found It*' campaign. The idea is that I found new life in Christ."

After that, we talked about Jesus and about the campaign. However, as I started to ask her if she wanted to pray with me to receive Christ as her personal Savior and Lord, her husband interrupted. He had just come home and was more than ready to eat.

She asked, "Could you send your materials home with Kimmy?" Of course, I agreed.

The next day, her daughter brought in a college yearbook that had a picture of me playing in a freshmen team basketball game. In those days, colleges had freshman teams. Most freshmen players didn't make the varsity until their sophomore year. I was no exception.

Her husband was a senior when I was a freshman, but it wasn't until my sophomore year that I joined. One day, after this call, he and I met. We talked about brothers that we both knew and some of the crazy things for which our fraternity was known. This certainly was a surprise.

The real reason the Lord orchestrated this call concerned her pregnancy. She was due any day. Her delivery, a caesarian section, did not go as planned. Her baby was fine, but she felt terrible afterward. The next time we met in school, she looked very pale and weak. I asked her what happened, but she didn't know. I promised to pray for her, which she seemed to appreciate.

After praying that night for her, the doctors decided to reopen the surgery site to see if they could find the problem. They did! Somehow, an unnoticed sponge was left inside her body when they closed her up. Apparently, the sponges were miscounted. What the sponge was doing to her system, I don't know, but whatever it was, it wasn't good.

Good news followed, thankfully. The doctors corrected the problem, and she recovered very quickly. She looked much better the next time we met. She thanked me for praying, and I thanked the Lord for the result. This strange occurrence had a great ending. Apparently, the Lord wanted her to not only hear about Jesus but to have someone pray for her as well. I was not sorry for calling the right number for the wrong person. It's obvious to me now that the person that answered was the right one after all.

I thank God for my years at that school, especially the unexpected wrong number. It was another great way to observe this truth—the Lord works in strange ways.

CHAPTER 7

The Chronicles of Narnia Play

The answers to prayer presented in this story happened in the spring of 1977. I was teaching a mentally gifted fifth-grade class in an Orange County, CA, school. Being familiar with *The Chronicles of Narnia*, it occurred to me that my class would enjoy the stories. They did, they loved them. I thank God for C. S. Lewis.

Some Christian students in my class explained the Christian meaning of the stories to their classmates when they were at recess. Their parents, not I, had explained the meaning of the stories as they read them to their children at home.

An area pastor, whose child was in my class, didn't like us reading *The Chronicles of Narnia*. I told him that I didn't understand. I would have thought that, as a pastor, he'd be praying for me and the kids; many Christian parents were. He said, "Well, I think the Bible is okay, but I like *The Chariots of the Gods* better." Really!

That convinced me that the Lord had led me to read the stories. I hadn't yet encountered pastors teaching from sources other than the Bible. His chosen book had nothing to do with the true *Echod Elohim*.

The adjective *Echod* in Hebrew is a pluralistic word for *one*. A good example is five fingers make up one hand. Elohim is the most popular name for God in the Old Testament. It also is a plural word which means *three degrees of personality*. In short, it speaks of God in three persons. It is the name of the only true God.

Was I the only one in the country reading those amazing stories to their classes? No, many Christian teachers across the country were. That was a miracle in itself. Obviously, the idea really came from the Lord, which He was sharing with many other teachers. I'm not arrogant enough to believe that they got the idea from me, but I definitely didn't get it from anyone else. It was an outgrowth of the "Jesus Movement" revival of the late '60s and '70s.

In reading the stories with my own children, I began to think about sharing the stories with my class. I went forward with the project, and it worked out very well; so well, in fact, that the idea of a play came to mind.

My only involvement in a play was playing the part of Joseph in our church Christmas play in 1959 and 1960. Joseph had no lines at all, he just sat there. That was my kind of role. The only downer was that my mom complained both years that my big toe was sticking up in the air, as my dad's would often do. In fact, I never knew it was happening until she mentioned it. It wasn't any big deal to me, but I remember thinking, "She would notice that."

With absolutely no play experience, trying to show these kids how to act, even emote, was a challenge. Directing a play was not in my repertoire. As far as I was concerned, succeeding in doing that would be a miracle. Still, it might work to the glory of God. Therefore, one day, I asked a very bright student to rewrite *The Lion, the Witch and the Wardrobe* into a play form. What she did was outstanding!

The entire class was involved by joining various committees, each with its own purpose. Those who didn't want a role in the play helped with drawing and painting large paper scenes. Others helped with changing the scenes during performances. Still, others copied the final draft for the players. It was an entire class effort. Their parents provided the costumes.

When it came to choosing students to play the various parts, problems occurred. I tried to match the characters with the students who would fit perfectly for the many parts. That went very well until we came to the six major roles.

At first, I let the kids vote on the students they thought would be best for those parts. That was a big mistake. They picked the most popular students, one of whom did not fit her elected role well. Therefore, changes in her role had to be made, which didn't sit well with her or her friends.

Today, I may have been chastened for not being sensitive to her self-esteem. Self-esteem does not guarantee a great result. My responsibility was to make casting decisions, which was the best course to take. Therefore, the change was made. Once all the roles were given to those that could play them best, the cast was incredible.

However, that one major role change was with a student whom the class voted to play one of the story's leading heroines. Instead of that part, she was perfect for a different leading role, the "White Witch." Now that was a real change!

Going from the role of a heroine to an evil witch was also not appreciated by her parents, which I thoroughly understood. However, good actors can take on roles which are the opposite of their personal character. It was obvious that she would take the role very seriously. She played her role perfectly, even better than my expectations. After the first performance, the decision was confirmed, and her parents agreed. She was great, as were the other cast members.

At our school, we had a stage that was set up as a theater-in-the-round. The first of our several performances were for the lower grades. It was fun to watch the younger students running to each scene. The upper grade students just shifted their bodies. In all, it was a big hit.

I asked my principal if we could put on the play for the parents and local residents. He said it wouldn't work at our school but we could try to get the junior-high stage for that purpose. He received the okay, and we went ahead with it. When we publicly announced the performance, there was enough interest to reserve two nights to do it. It was a full house both nights.

In one respect, it was a nightmare. Apparently, no one at the junior high had ever used the scene holders, which were extremely stiff. They hung down from above on a horizontal support. We attached two paper scenes, back-to-back, to each holder. Supposedly, when the curtain was closed, we would be able to just rotate the scenes. Simple! At least that was the plan.

Unfortunately, the holders refused to cooperate both nights. Once the curtain was closed, I had to pound the holders with a two-by-four to get them to turn. It sounded as if a war was going on backstage. The second night, the board broke in half in the process. We wound up with my wife, several taller students, and me holding up the scenes. We even made certain the audience would not see our hands. It worked well enough that it didn't distract from the play; at least it solved the noise problem. However, a little bit of oil could have solved both.

I had prayed for great results, and the Lord delivered. Everyone played their part to the hilt. That same year, the local high school performed *The Music Man*. A number of parents had seen both plays and liked the acting in our play better. It was nice to hear, but the Lord did it. The kids did their best; it was their play all the way.

My fifth-grade gifted students may not have realized it, but the Lord had led them to experience something they would never forget. Every one of them was incredible.

In never having directed a play before, this was a miracle. Little did I know that this play experience would serve an even greater purpose for an evangelistic play a year later. However, what I learned from the class play was this: if one is looking for healthy self-esteem—it's best to let the Lord take over.

"And whatever you do, do it heartily, as to the Lord and not to men," (Colossians 3:23 NKJV)

CHAPTER 8

The Christmas Play

In 1970, my dad had researched new developments in Georgia and Florida that offered affordable golf. Once he retired, they sold their house and moved to Deltona, Florida. He hoped to play golf several times a week, and Deltona fit the bill.

Dad enjoyed that for a little less than four years before passing away. Several years after Dad's passing, Mom was getting tired of the three-bedroom house and yard. During our visit with her, she suggested that we buy her house. She knew of a condo, perfect for her and close to several friends. We agreed and, in the summer of 1978, moved to Deltona.

I was hired at a nearby school to teach emotionally handi-capped children in the fall. I had two years of prior experience teaching Special Education, but this would become the hardest year of my entire teaching career. My students came from broken homes, non-English-speaking families or a nearby institution for orphans and wards of the state. My eight students ranged in age from nine to sixteen. It was very difficult, to say the least. Only a few of them could read above a third-grade level. The oldest students were lower than that. The sixteen-year-olds had a first-grade reading level.

My wife was hired as my assistant, which was a good thing for a while. On Friday mornings, she would make a great breakfast for the kids, which was followed by an entertaining movie or a field trip. Soon, the kids began to call us Mom and Dad. My wife and I had worked very well together. Our Mom-and-Dad approach provided some stability for those kids. We felt like we had a ministry and were making headway. However, a problem arose with that arrangement.

The district had a rule that forbid a spouse to work under the authority of another. Therefore, she had to be switched to another class. Fortunately, my new assistant was a Christian and an acquaintance of ours. She was a big help to me in continuing the program.

However, I knew they needed much more than I or the school district could give them. I had worked for a school in New York State that combined the basics with vocational training. The students there had the same problems that my Florida students had. However, once they got into the vocational training, they worked harder in learning the basics. It was a great approach. Our Florida school didn't have that program then; I hope they do now.

Thankfully, the Lord provided a series of miracles in our life outside of school. Our first pastor, Ron, had shared a Christmas story he had written called "Inside the Inn." He had sent his story to a Christian periodical, but they rejected it. However, before putting it back into his filing cabinet, he read it to us during Sunday school. After hearing it, I asked him if he would give his story to me to convert to a play. The C.S. Lewis play went well, and this was an opportunity to do something similar with his story. Perhaps it could be used for evangelistic purposes.

With his permission, I converted it. It was a fictional Christmas story about the inn where Christ was born. It centered on an inn-keeper's daughter, who tried desperately to find someone within the inn to change places with Joseph and Mary. Her concern was that the stable was not a proper place for the birth of a newborn. As she went to the different rooms, each person had a different excuse for not consenting. They were the same excuses that people also use to reject Christ today. Using Scripture or biblical principles, I prayerfully wrote songs to specifically correspond with each excuse.

Our California church had a terrible split that spring and finally ceased to exist. Since we were moving, I saved the play until we found a good church in the area of our new community.

We did find a good church. Once settled in, I asked my new pastor if he would be interested in the play. He was not only interested but very excited about the idea. I ran all of the music and the play past our music director. When he said, "Let's do it," the music director arranged the songs for our choir and the pianist. He did incredible arrangements in connecting each song to each excuse. It was much better than what I could have done.

We then assembled a great cast and put a team together to build the scenes. I was amazed! Those scenes looked as if professionals had made them. Everything was set to go for our first Christmas performance; at least, it was what we thought.

I'm not sure which was harder that year, teaching emotionally handicapped students or directing a group of adults in an evangelistic play. The class had settled down, but the play's cast was like herding cats. Everyone had their opinion of what I should change. They passed those opinions on to my wife, sometimes in the form of complaints. Many of the complaints centered on the music, which I had expected.

Most Christmas performances have the usual carols such as "Away in the Manger," but this one didn't. And, to add even more confusion to it, the music was different from anything they had heard or had to learn. That was my doing. Since it was an evangelistic play, I felt the lyrics had to be clearly understood. The songs were not only from Bible verses, principles, and descriptions, but there was also a Jewish flair to them. All of the characters were Jews. Once the cast got into the evangelistic mission of the play, they caught on to the music and its meaning.

It was definitely not the more contemporary Christian rock, which had begun to be played in churches around that time. From my jazz background, it did have a few upbeat tunes. Though there was one cast member with other ideas about the music, nothing was changed. I believed, in my heart, that God had written the play and music through me to glorify His Son. Naturally, I understood the purpose.

Another problem, also my doing, was not letting the cast know the ending. Beside my wife and me, only one choir member knew it. The ending made the play make sense. We felt it would be better if the other cast members experienced it as the first audience would.

By the time of the first performance, the cast members had complained to my wife about almost everything. They totally didn't understand the point, but they couldn't have. Thankfully, my wife stood with me because she also knew the overall evangelistic plan.

I think it's fair to say that most Christmas plays are generally more traditional than evangelistic. However, what better time is there to be evangelistic than Christmas? In any event, the play was definitely not traditional.

The part the cast didn't know happened after the innkeeper's daughter began to wonder aloud whether the child in the manger was the Messiah. She vocally wondered what the inn's guests would do once confronted with the fact that Jesus was the Messiah. What excuses would they use then to reject Him—their promised Savior and Lord?

After considering the excuses, a cross appeared on a screen behind her with the chilling sound of the spikes being hammered. We created that effect by clanging two railroad spikes together. It was too realistic, but it was good! If anyone fell asleep during the play, it was sure to awaken them.

At end of the play, a woman in the choir stepped out to ask, "Hey, mister, what's a cross doing in a Christmas play?" I replied, "Without the cross, there would be no Christmas." That started a dialogue on what Christ's finished work on the cross meant to our salvation by faith in Him alone. The message followed with an invitation to receive the Lord.

The first performance succeeded with many conversions to Christ. It also reached the heart of the cast members. Everyone came to me afterward to apologize for their complaints. Although being pleased with their attitude and apologies, my wife had a different take on it. She said, "They complained to me but apologized to you? Great!" I promised to convey that message to them in a kind way later, which I did. Many followed up with apologies to her, which she appreciated. After that first performance, thankfully, there were no more complaints.

That first performance was at our church in De Leon Springs. Although our church was forty-five minutes away, a pastor from

Deltona invited us to make our second performance at his church. Many of the members were my mother's age, which at the time was seventy-two. That gave me an idea.

We invited my mom and friends of her choice to attend the performance. They also needed to hear of the Lord's finished work on the cross on our behalf. Although, not knowing our motive, Mom was very happy to oblige. Our hope was that my mom and one or two of the others would receive Christ that night. The Holy Spirit came through with His message of the saving grace of Jesus Christ by faith alone.

"For by grace you have been saved through faith; it is the gift of God, not of works lest anyone should boast." (Ephesians 2:8-9 NKJV)

CHAPTER 9

The "Inside the Inn" Play Miracles

D uring my growing up years, my mother supervised the nursery during the morning service at our home church. The sermon was piped in through a loudspeaker in the nursery. However, she was always so busy, it's doubtful she heard anything about salvation. I can't remember hearing much about salvation either.

My mother was about as good a mom as my two sisters and I could have. However, after my conversion, I wondered whether she, a staunch Presbyterian, really knew the Lord. Therefore, from day one of my becoming a Christian, I witnessed the gospel to her. It wasn't an easy task. When asked what she believed about Jesus, she would say, "I believe what the Presbyterians believe!" If that followed with, "What do they believe?" she would reply, "What I believe!" She was a pro at circular reasoning. Obviously, that was cause for concern.

She knew very little about the Bible. She had once told me that Jesus died so we could live, which, although true, stumped me. As a youth, I thought she meant that if Jesus hadn't died, there would be no human life left on the earth. She had learned that line in her Lutheran church, but I'm not sure she really understood it. At the time, I was too young to question what it meant.

Later, I found that she definitely didn't understand the cross or the virgin birth. She couldn't see why being born of a virgin or Jesus dying on the cross was necessary. She even admitted that she didn't understand why He had to resurrect to give us life. She felt God could do whatever He wanted to do, and He would be just in doing it. I agreed with her that He is just. That was His reason for carrying out His plan for man's redemption. However, He never told us to adjust His plan to meet our personal specifications. Unfortunately, many people do.

From her point of view, God should only save those who follow the Ten Commandments. It's possible she was never taught that one had to also be born without a sin nature to live a sinless life. Jesus Christ had to be born without a sin nature if he was to accomplish His mission perfectly. Nor did she know that following all of the commandments of the Mosaic Law sinlessly was His prerequisite for messianic eligibility. Jesus met those specifications. He was born without a sin nature and did live a perfectly sinless life according to the Mosaic Law.

Obviously, no one had done it before Him and no one has done it since. He left his position as the second person of the triune God to humble himself by becoming a man. He was the only one found worthy to go to the cross in our place. He was our sacrificial lamb.

The Law, on the other hand, was never given to save anyone. It could only condemn! Adam, perfect at first, started out without a sin nature. He had a chance to live without sin. However, he wasn't born, he was created. Because of his sin, he acquired a sin nature. It is from that one man that all human beings have a sin nature, passed down from every father to his children.

This is why Jesus had to be conceived by the Holy Spirit. It was imperative that He did not have a sin nature. He was the only exception in history to be born without one. The only way He would have received one was to give in to sin as the created Adam did. Thankfully, He didn't.

Something that is often overlooked is the matter of fallen angels. They were led out of heaven by the old serpent, the devil, God's highest created angel. Through his superego, he became the evil one, our enemy. He and his followers were then expelled from heaven. It's thought to have happened before the creation of the universe, which makes sense.

God then created His highest being next to Him, Adam. He was made in the image of the triune God, just as we have been.

Afterward, God created Eve from Adam's body. Satan and his network, intent on destroying God's creation, went after God's two highest created beings.

He knew that Adam would not give in to him, but he might if Eve did. Therefore, he first came to Eve in the form of a beautiful serpent, which may have been one of her favorite creatures. Once she was deceived and ate the fruit of the knowledge of good and evil, she neither felt nor exhibited any change in her personality. Because the fruit was good to eat, she deceived Adam. When he noticed that she didn't die, his deception was easy. He doubted God's Word!

From that point on, everyone's sin nature has been passed down through a father. The sin nature, now part of Adam, was not part of Eve. Why? She was created from part of Adam's body. He said of her:

> *"This is now bone of my bones and flesh of my flesh; She shall be called Woman, Because she was taken out of Man."* (Genesis 2:23 NKJV)

They were both perfect until the fall. After the fall, she became a sinner, but her sin nature was still Adam's. The two were literally one flesh. That may explain why she didn't feel or look different to Adam until he sinned. Once his deception was complete, it was then their eyes were opened. They felt the evil difference inside them and were afraid.

God, knowing that no man or woman could ever go to heaven with a sin nature or even just one sin, told Adam and later Abraham, Isaac, Jacob, Moses, and Joseph that He would send His Holy One, the Messiah, to die in our place. He gave Moses the Law only to keep His chosen people close to Him. It was never to save or qualify them for salvation.

God knew that a man could not save himself, and therefore, only He could supply the remedy. Jesus, the Father's Son, had to become the sacrificial lamb to die in our place. He came to erase the penalty of all sin at the cross. Jesus, the second Adam, succeeded in doing what the first Adam couldn't. He qualified by living the perfectly sinless life.

From the beginning, the Jews found it very difficult to keep the law. However, they all knew that God would one day provide the Messiah to pay the entire penalty of their sins. Their leaders definitely should have been ready to receive God's only Son, their Messiah. His triumphal entry into Jerusalem happened on the exact prophesied year and day. Yet, they scolded Him for accepting their praise. The exact words the people used were also prophesied.

We see from the OT that the Jews knew the Law would not save them. For that reason, they gave up following it. Every now and then they would come back to it but their heart wasn't in it. They were afraid of God and didn't want to hear Him speak. The truth is they wanted to do things their own way. Does that sound familiar?

Everything said previous to this paragraph was explained to my mom. However, nothing I said gave her any reason to receive the Lord. She was condemning herself without knowing it. It's easy to deceive ourselves to think that we are good enough for God. She wouldn't have been the first. She still thought she was good enough to make the cut, which doesn't exist! Clearly, we had to find another way to make the gospel understandable to her. That was our continual prayer.

Finally, one night, while trying again to explain God's plan of salvation, I became frustrated. That's where the Lord entered the conversation. I asked her if she knew anything about the last words or phrases of Christ on the cross. She said yes, but one had always bothered her.

I thought she would say, "My God, My God, why hast thou forsaken me?" That one would have been easy to explain. Once a believer understands that Jesus was quoting the beginning of Psalm 22, he will see that it's a proof text that HE WAS AND IS THE MESSIAH. Jesus was quoting it for the Pharisees, Sadducees, priests, and scribes to hear. Hear what? They had unknowingly set the stage for their Messiah to go to the cross. It was actually necessary for their salvation. Unfortunately, they didn't understand what they should have known.

Psalm 22 clearly shows the thoughts of the Messiah on the cross. It was written one thousand years prior to His birth and nine hundred years before crucifixion became the Roman method of execution.

However, that wasn't the one that confused her. It was Jesus stating, "It is finished!" I was really glad she said that. It is this statement which declares that He earned our salvation for us. It could also be explained easily, but it necessitated more detail, which would cover the other things she didn't understand. This was an open door, or so I thought.

I conveyed this to Mom: "Jesus was proclaiming that our salvation was finished. In going to the cross in our place, He had paid the full price for the sins of the entire world. In fulfilling that prophecy, He had erased sin's penalty, which is eternal damnation in hell. If we believe in Him by faith alone, salvation is ours, which can never be lost." I also told her that nothing, including good works, can add to it or save us in any way. He paid it all! His redemptive mission was finished at the cross. Therefore, He proclaimed, "It is finished."

We then went to the book of John, *"For God so loved the world, that he gave his only Son, that whoever believes in him should not perish but have eternal life."* (John 3:16 ESV)

Jesus meant that we are saved by grace through faith alone; good works are not mentioned anywhere in that verse. And, since He had paid the sins of the entire world, He offered redemption to everyone.

A person must receive Jesus Christ to be saved. This is the unequivocal truth of the gospel. Anyone trying to be saved through works of any kind or by any other way must be judged by the Mosaic Law. That judgment will happen at the end of Christ's upcoming thousand-year reign. That's a losing situation for the unrepentant sinner. After physical death, he, not God, sends his eternal spirit, to hell. It's the default position for those who reject such a great salvation.

We then discussed the real problem for the nonbeliever. Since all people, with the exception of Jesus, have a sin nature, right there we lose. But if we didn't have a sin nature, it only takes one sin to be guilty of all; hence Adam and Eve. I imagine the average person, believer or nonbeliever, probably commits over a million sins in a lifetime. Therefore, with the exception of the sinless Jesus, even if someone had a very low number of sins, say one to one thousand, he or she must be found guilty. Sinners have to face eternal punishment if dying without Christ. We all know there is no one who committed only one sin.

Scripture tells us, *"For all have sinned, and come short of the glory of God."* (Romans 3:23 KJV) In other words, all of us were condemned at birth, just by having a sin nature. Without Christ's finished work on the cross, all human beings would have to be judged by the Law. Thankfully, His sacrifice changed all of that, but few today seem to know or want it.

Most believe, as I do, that children are exempt until the age of accountability. That moment probably differs with each one of us. Childlike faith, which Jesus said all adults must have, gives us a clue to that belief. Children wholeheartedly believe in God when they learn of Him.

Whenever I consider the lost, I think, how tragic! Every person could avoid everlasting punishment by receiving Christ's offer of eternal life with Him. Most people have not or will not accept Jesus as their savior and Lord. It must sadden Jesus. His offer of salvation is open to all. He loves each person specifically.

However, God cannot allow people to live with Him for eternity with sin still imputed to them. He hates sin in His presence. Why? Sin would still have to be paid in full, which is impossible for unrepentant sinners. In heaven, they would still be sinners and may turn against Him. Look only to what the demons did. Angels, who knew no sin, rebelled and followed Satan. God could not let that happen through fallen human beings in heaven. We had to experience our sin on earth and its forgiveness. His righteousness must be imputed to those who are His for all time. Remember, God created us in His image; angels were not. They will serve us.

It is also a sin to believe there is a better way to eternal life with God other than the sacrifice of His own perfect Son on the cross. Think about that. It's a slap in the Lord's face. He paid it all, but we think we can somehow work off our sins? Remember, we are talking about eternity here. To neglect such a great salvation, by trying to do it some other way, has eternal consequences.

That doesn't mean the good works, which God has chosen for us, aren't important. They are, but they have nothing to do with salvation. They are definitely important to our relationship with Christ. They bring us into a deeper understanding of the awesomeness of God. Works are meant for God's glorification, which He achieves through us. However, His works are part of our sanctification process. They are meant to bolster our faith and spiritual growth with Him.

Our works were prepared beforehand by Him that we should walk in them (Eph 2:10). I suggested to Mom that she think about this: if there was another way, would Jesus, the second person of the eternal God, become a man to die for us? No! But since He did, it proves He is the only way to heaven. And, it's free to anyone who would take it by His gift of faith. He paid a horrible price for us, but He did it. The redemption of believers was now accomplished. That is what He meant when he said, *"It is finished."* (John 19:30 KJV)

Mom was quiet for a few seconds. Then, instead of the usual debate about faith and works, she said, "So that's what He meant when He said, 'It is finished'?" I said yes. She was finally getting it. Though she still wasn't ready to pray with me, there was reason to hope.

At that second play, a man who had prayed with me to receive Christ told me that something seemed to hit his hand, which resulted in him losing all desire to smoke. Wow! That was amazing. He told me to pray that he would never smoke again, and I did. That first miracle was a good sign that the Lord was honoring our mission, which was really all His from the beginning.

My mother attended the play at the little Deltona church with three friends. After the invitation, she also prayed to receive the Lord. She even told her friends later that she had prayed the prayer with me, which was a witness of her new life in Christ. Witnessing is a sign of the indwelling Holy Spirit in the believer's life. Her friends did not receive the Lord but said the play did give them something to think about.

I wish she had told me directly that night. I didn't find out about my mom's salvation prayer until almost two years later. I realize now, though, it wasn't her fault, it was mine. When I asked who had prayed with me to receive the Lord, many hands went up, Mom's included. However, I was concentrating on just counting the hands, not their owners. Apparently, she thought I had seen her hand among the others and didn't feel the need to tell me.

Almost two years later, I was talking to her about Jesus during a phone conversation, and somehow the subject of eternal security came up. She said, "Why are you talking to me now as if I weren't saved? I know where I'm going when I die." I said, "When did that happen?" She replied, "It happened when you gave the invitation during the play at the church in Deltona! I prayed with you to receive the Lord. You asked those who prayed to raise their hand, and I did!"

Wow! Leave it to me to miss that wonderful blessing! Tears filled my eyes. God had answered my prayer for my mother. She was seventy-two then, and at the age of ninety-five, she went to be with Him forever. Mom's redemption had finally happened, and I will definitely see her again.

"Not by works of righteousness, which we have done, but according to His mercy He saved us!" (Titus 3:5 NKJV)

CHAPTER 10

Flashback: The Straitjacket

The first performance of the play had gone very well. The next two were total opposites; one with great results, as related in the last chapter, and the other with few attending and no conversions. The latter church was located in a little town known for the cult of astrology. That reminded me of my mother-in-law's conversion, which is important to share.

When I received the Lord, I read a book that featured many great testimonies. One stood out to me for a special reason. It was a story of a man trapped into the deeper workings of astrology. It concerned the end goal of astrology. He claimed it was to coerce ardent followers to commit suicide. If true, most people who just dabble in it do not know it, but others who have gone deep either do or did.

Pastor Ron had said that astrology is the world's oldest satanic religion. That makes sense since our enemy's evil ministry is to keep people from receiving Christ. What better way to do it than by promoting suicide. Therefore, from that man's testimony above, I could believe it. Whether it is or isn't the oldest, it's definitely satanic. Why? Not only is it deceptive, but it draws people away from trusting the Lord for their life.

When the government of Israel was a theocracy, God ruled Israel through judges. They consulted the Lord for everything. But, the people rebelled against them. They didn't want the Lord telling them what to do; they wanted a man to rule over them. God gave them King Saul.

The Spirit of the Lord was placed upon him, but he refused to follow God as instructed. Instead, King Saul disobeyed the Lord. God became so angry with him that He took the Holy Spirit from the king. He then placed the Holy Spirit upon David, a man after God's own heart. The end of Saul's life explains the problem. Saul consulted an astrologer, instead of the Lord or the Lord's prophet the day before his demise. Saul's end was not a good one.

The same thing could have happened to my mother-in-law. Along with blindly accepting the cultic religion, she was drinking herself to death. That compounded her problem.

This is what the Lord says about astrology:

> *"Thou art wearied in the multitude of thy counsels. Let now the astrologers, the stargazers, the monthly prognosticators, stand up, and save thee from these things that shall come upon thee. Behold, they shall be as stubble; the fire shall burn them; they shall not deliver themselves from the power of the flame:"* (Isaiah 47:13–14 KJV)

Yet, today, people reject Jesus but love to follow astrologers, which cannot save anyone. My wife and her mother were once in that camp. Of the two, it was Donna's mother who really studied it. Like everyone else, she started by reading her horoscope in the paper for fun. As she got more into it, every day, she not only checked her horoscope but read from many books about the religion. Her day would start with that and end with her drinking herself to drunkenness, which fortunately didn't take very long.

After the Lord changed my life, she began to call me to see why and how I stopped drinking. I would give my testimony, but because of her drinking, she never remembered it. Finally, I asked if I could send her a professional, a close friend of our family, and she agreed.

Our friend, Phil, was a recovering alcoholic, a director of a rehab center and later a pastor. He had done a complete turnaround once the Lord called him. Phil was our neighbor when I was studying jazz and jamming with local musicians in our home. His children seemed to enjoy listening to it.

However, Phil knew me before I was saved and recognized that I had a problem with alcohol. Although I didn't know it, He and his family were praying for my family's conversion.

Thankfully, it happened about a year and a half later. After our conversion, my wife said he was the person my mother-in-law needed. Once we were in the fold, I contacted him to relate our testimony, which Phil was thrilled to hear. He invited us to attend one of his church services, which we did and liked it very much. Afterward, we had lunch with his family to discuss my mother-in-law's problem. He confirmed that both issues, astrology and drinking, were dangerous and didn't go together well.

Phil told me to set up an appointment with her. When she agreed to meet with him, I pleaded with her to stay sober that day. We wanted her to hear what had happened to change Phil's life. Our hope was that the Lord would also change hers. She promised she would stay sober, but she didn't.

I once read a newspaper headline that still makes me laugh. It read, *"You can't always trust criminals, they sometimes lie."* No kidding! I should have sent that to Jay Leno. If the word criminals were changed to drunks or users, it would still be true.

As it would turn out, it was better that she didn't listen to me. She was a mess when Phil arrived. He wasn't there long before Donna's father agreed to have her committed to the rehab center. That night, she was admitted, in a straitjacket.

That was the best thing that could have happened to her. While she was confined, she asked for a Bible. Within a few days, she surrendered to Christ and her life turned around. From that day to her death, she remained strong in her faith and never took another drink.

At the request of her husband, she went through the AA program at Phil's rehab center, which helped her to meet a few Christian friends. It really didn't take much to keep her from drinking, but it did take months before the Lord opened her eyes to the dangers of astrology.

Finally, she replaced her astrology literature with the Bible and books about the Bible. We even bought her the Bible on cassettes, which she really loved. My father-in-law did also, but it took a lot to get him to understand belief in Christ by faith alone. His religious upbringing did not agree with that. On the other hand, he was well aware of our changed lives, something he never witnessed in his former church. But then, he hadn't attended any church service of his denomination since his marriage. If he did, it wasn't for very long. However, he did attend church with his wife once she was saved.

I will always remember my mother-in-law's experience with the Lord because it was in close proximity to mine. Once she put her faith and trust in Jesus, she never looked back. After being convinced to follow and trust the Lord for her life, good things happened to the entire family. She always thanked God for what He did to change all of our lives.

Her changed life brought our family closer together but the important thing was that she was set free. Praise God, His wonders to perform. There would be no more straitjacket of the soul, once she knew the truth—she was free indeed.

"And you shall know the truth, and the truth shall make you free." (John 8:32 NKJV)

CHAPTER 11

That Night at the Jail

When we took our play to the church in that cultic area, only fifteen people showed up. It went over well with them, but no one had invited any of their nonbelieving friends. Perhaps the church pastor and leadership misunderstood our evangelistic purpose. That was understandable since it was a Christmas play. Like so many churches, they probably didn't expect it.

We were told, coming in, the eyes of its residents were totally blinded to the truth. The low attendance was proof of that. On the way home, I had feelings of despair for that area. Whenever I am in that kind of town, the oppression can be felt.

However, once we arrived home, something wonderful happened that turned my heart's sadness to joy. We received a phone call which told me something miraculous had resulted from the play. A play attendee that night was a co-worker with one of our actors. He could see another venue for us. He contacted his co-worker to ask if we would consider a performance for three different groups at their place of employment, the county jail.

Of course, I was really up for that, but not everyone else was, including my family. Later, it became obvious that I had to sell it to our cast. Very few of the cast members liked the idea. They were a little nervous about three performances in a jail. My wife, Donna, was also concerned, especially when one of the officers on duty told us to remember, "These men didn't get here by singing too loud in church." Enough said!

Two miracles happened that night, one involving an inmate and the other involving my wife. I'll relate my wife's condition first, which will be followed by the hardened inmate's. The two ensuing miracles became intertwined. Both were incredible!

When Donna and I first met, we were both heavy smokers. She didn't smoke as much as I did, but in her mind, cigarettes were her little friends. Of all forms of satanic deception, smoking is definitely at the top of the list. To make matters worse, although God took away my desire to smoke, she couldn't stop. She tried for three years, but she didn't even last two weeks before returning to them. It was understandable; my past had its share of two-week abstentions.

For three years, I had begged the Lord to do what He had done for me—*completely remove her desire to smoke.* Socially, it was hard to visit other Christian friends. None of them smoked. She would have to excuse herself and go outside when we stayed too long. We never stayed overnight with anyone for the same reason. After church, she would immediately light up in the car, which nauseated us a little, but I tried not to complain.

After three years of praying for her to quit, I became resigned to the fact it was too hard for her. And, it didn't seem to be a priority with the Lord either. Of course, I hoped I was wrong. We are never to bring God down to our level of understanding. Remember, all things are possible with Him.

A few days before the three performances, she still wasn't excited about attending. She was apprehensive about the entire idea. She was mainly concerned about the amount of time the three plays would take. If it was too long, where could she go to smoke? It's a jail! She couldn't go outside; we would be locked in for the duration.

Fortunately, after much prayer, she decided to go. That excited me because we needed her, and she didn't disappoint. She used her gift of helps by making sandwiches for the cast to enjoy between per-formances. That sounded good to me. She finally had peace about what we were going to do and said so. She said she knew the Lord would do something great.

Her willing attitude pleased me; that was until she heard the officer give me the warning when we first arrived. More importantly, he also warned me to watch out for a particular inmate who would be attending the last performance. At that point, she became uneasy, but still went through with her mission to feed our cast and help in any way she could.

Apparently, the man to avoid was really mean and could easily become violent. Donna became afraid for me and begged me to listen to what the officer had said about him. She didn't have to beg, I was totally on board with her. I wanted no part of him. Even with my military training, I wasn't one to get into fights. In fact, because of my training, that was more of a reason not to. The majority of veterans understand that.

The first performance was for the men with lighter sentences, which went very well. That was followed by a performance for the women, which also went well. The third performance was for the hardened criminals, which, at first, was a challenge. As the dangerous-offenders group made their way in, the officer pointed out the inmate to avoid.

The officer was right, he did get ornery. As I was going through my preaching spiel, he mocked me the entire time. What happened next could have been only the Lord's doing.

Just before the invitation to receive the Lord, I walked over to him, looked him straight in the eye and said, "You need Jesus Christ in your life more than anyone in this room." You could hear a pin drop. For some reason, concern for my safety was not important, which would be up to the Lord. It was imperative for me to say that!

All of a sudden, he stopped mocking. He stood there staring at me as if dumbfounded that I would dare confront him. I didn't realize what was happening until, suddenly, he began to weep. Unscathed, I gratefully walked back to my original position and gave an invitation to receive the Lord. Those that wanted salvation prayed with me, word for word, to receive Jesus.

After the prayer, as heads were still bowed, I asked those who had prayed with me to raise their hands. His hand went up first. God had acted in a way no one expected.

Unfortunately, because these men were the more hardened group, I was not able to talk with him afterward. However, our pastor did address the group and gave them some literature on the next steps for growing in faith. He told them to consider our church as theirs. I don't know if anything ever came of that, but that night, the Lord's nudge to confront this inmate concerning his spiritual condition was overwhelming. Although having been told by the officer not to rile him, the Lord's perfect peace couldn't be ignored. And, He didn't disappoint. This inmate's repentant response to Jesus was truly a miracle!

Meanwhile, my wife, cringing in fear, urgently began to pray as I approached him. Suddenly, the Lord's peace settled on her in a similar way. At the same time, He not only answered her prayer for me, but he also answered my three-year prayer for her. She lost all desire to smoke at that very moment. She was excited to tell me that afterward. I thought of the verse, *"Why are you fearful, O you of little faith?"* (Matthew 8:26 NKJV)

I had given up, but the Lord hadn't. She never smoked again.

Several of the new believers from the first group, the ones who were not serious offenders, helped us take down the scenes and all of our props. They also helped us take them to our truck, while, at the same time, thanking us for coming. One young man's release was in four days. He was especially grateful and said he couldn't wait to tell his wife and family that he had prayed to receive the Lord. It was something she had always wanted him to do. That was an extra blessing.

During those three performances, fifty-six inmates, both men and women, prayed to receive Christ. That was about a third of all that attended. The final play was again held in our church. More conversions also occurred that night. In all of the performances that week, 156 attendees received Jesus Christ as their Savior and Lord. It's exciting to think I'll see them again in heaven.

Those miracles were definitely some of the greatest and most enjoyable of my life. The sadness had turned to joy in ways that I will never forget. His peace that passes all understanding did the trick.

Of all of the conversions that week, the miracle with the hardened criminal, and especially the way the Lord freed my wife from smoking, brought joy to our lives. Later, learning of my mom's conversion made it complete, even though it took two years.

That night at the jail, of all places, reminded me that God is so good! Somehow, that seems like an understatement. He's great!

The joy of the Lord is your strength! (Nehemiah 8:10 NKJV)

CHAPTER **12**

God Calling!

his next miracle occurred at a seminary in Maryland in the summer of 1979. I had been accepted to attend the seminary but
could not find a supporting job. We had been staying at the seminary
all summer. However, I also was accepted at a different seminary in
Wilkinsburg, Pennsylvania, near my home town of Pittsburgh. They
found a job for me, which made it seem like a good fit. However, we
had to go back to the seminary in Maryland to get our things still in
the dorm.

An unexpected phone call concerning a family member startled us. By that I mean, we weren't supposed to have been where we
got the call. We should have been in the Pittsburgh area, where our
families would have called if they needed us. This is what happened
that day.

My wife's grandmother was an interesting person. When we
met, I realized that she called the shots. She and her husband Hal got
along with me quite well. Once Grandma saw the change in me, she
gave it a while before she said anything. But, one night, when I was
witnessing to her and Donna's other grandmother, she said to me, "I
have met a lot of people that believe in God, but you are inspired."
Of course, that wasn't true. Christians may sound as if we are because
of Bible study and weekly teaching. Most people today know only a
little about God's Word.

Born-again Christians have the indwelling of the Holy Spirit.
He helps us to learn, understand, and share the gospel. Therefore,

whenever we share the Word of God with others, we may seem to be inspired. However, it is really the inspiration of the Holy Spirit speaking through us. Only the Word of God is truly inspired; we who spread the gospel aren't. Our job is to pass on God's inspired words to those who have never heard or understood them. Grandma showed enough understanding to ask for the faith to believe, but her religion may have kept her from actually doing it.

That trip to the seminary to get our personal items out of the dorm had to be done quickly, but for a different reason than we had envisioned. During one of my last trips to the parking lot, I decided to find an easier way to our car and back. That way was through the laundry room, a small room with an open entry at each end. The room was only about twenty yards from our car.

The laundry room also housed the only pay phone in the dorm. Those of us living in the dorm used it generally to call out. It was rare to receive a call. We had originally given that number to our extended families in case they needed to get in touch with us. Donna always contacted them first, anyway, if there was anything new to report. They liked that process. When we went to Pittsburgh to check out a different seminary, we let our families know we were there. We also gave them the number to call.

Donna wanted to wait until we were settled to explain the change to her parents. That was our plan, but the Lord had something else in mind. On my last trip from the car through the laundry room, the pay phone rang. I stopped dead in my tracks. For some reason known only to God, I knew it was my father-in-law calling to tell us that his mother had passed away. I hesitantly answered the phone to hear a very distraught and tearful man tell me exactly that.

It wasn't completely unexpected. She had a bad heart. However, we had recently talked with her before we went north. At that time, she seemed to be well.

We were planning to spend as little time as possible at the dorm, but the call changed our plans. As would be expected, my wife and kids were very upset. They had never experienced a death of a major relative. My wife called the Pittsburgh International Airport to get flight times to Seattle for the kids and her. I had to start work in only a few days; otherwise, I would have gone with them.

After making the airline reservations, we drove hurriedly to Pittsburgh International, arriving just in time for them to board. You could still do that in those days.

What really mattered was the way Donna's parents got through to us. How did I know it was my father-in-law calling? What are the odds of my in-laws calling that number, which would ring at the exact moment I was passing through the small laundry room? And it happened on a day when we had planned to get out of there as quickly as possible.

The bigger question is, what made me feel that it was not only my in-laws calling but that Grandma had passed away? As sad as it was, a miracle had happened. Donna's father had connected with us by calling that number. Donna and the kids could attend the funeral, and I could look for a place to live. That was another miracle, but I'll skip it for now.

This time, my in-laws called the wrong number, but the right person answered. To my way of thinking, it was once again—***God calling***.

*"Casting all your care upon Him, for He
cares for you"* (1 Peter 5:7 NKJV)

CHAPTER **13**

"It's a God Story, Son"

In 1987, we moved to Warrendale, Pennsylvania, north of Pittsburgh. The move was the beginning of a whole new career for me. It's been one that would continue in various ways for the next thirty years. Sadly, Donna would live only the first twelve of those years. However, she did have a miracle happen the year we moved to Warrendale.

I became a church bond broker for a Christian-based investment banking firm, but first had to study for the Series 7 Exam to get my broker's license. Although my dad always encouraged me to drop psychology and study business, that was the one profession that didn't appeal to me. It took a long time before accepting his advice. He would have been pleased if he were still alive.

The day of the test result was exciting. The exam wasn't easy, it's meant to eliminate candidates. To get the result, I needed to find a pay phone. There were few portable cell phones around then, and pay phones were still fairly easy to find.

I needed to walk a bit, anyway, and welcomed the chance; hospitals can be a downer. My wife was recovering from a repaired stomach bypass operation. After her arthritis was diagnosed, she had trouble keeping her weight down because of the medicine. In fact, she really put it on. That made her condition worse. It was very hard on her joints, which had deformed at a very rapid rate. To get her weight back to a level she could manage, she chose to have a bypass.

However, the original operation was connected too far down. Of course, we didn't know that. As Donna lost weight, she began to look younger and healthier. However, that didn't last long. Her body, over a period of six to eight months, could no longer live on her fat. There wasn't any left. Since the food was circumventing the intestinal system, no nutrition was getting into her body.

Soon, she began to look pale and weak. Suddenly, one day, she started acting strangely. Our doctor quickly sent her to a well-known specialist to determine the problem. Once the doctor realized her condition, he explained the procedure needed to repair the failed bypass. Her decision was a simple one, operate or perish.

The procedure to correct the botched bypass was successful, but an unforeseen problem occurred. A yeast infection on the tip of the central line took up residence in her body. However, a few days went by before the symptoms occurred. During that time, she seemed to be fine and recovering normally. She was awake and fairly lucid when I went to find a pay phone to see about my Series 7 Exam result.

If the exam result was positive, a meeting was set for later that day with a church board. After receiving the successful result, I went back to tell Donna the good news and to remind her that I had to leave for the meeting. She politely listened and smiled, it was obvious something was wrong. It appeared that she just needed sleep, which I suggested. It sounded good to her, and she fell asleep quickly.

I went on to meet with the church leaders about a bond issue. However, I became concerned about what may be happening with her. Normally, it would have been exhilarating just to make my first potential client presentation. The prospect that I now had my license and could finally do what church bond brokers do was exciting, but that was quelled by Donna's condition. She was in trouble!

After the meeting, I called the hospital to tell her how it went, only to be told that she was in ICU. If there was any excitement, it was very short-lived. My wife developed a high fever. She had gone into a coma. After returning to the hospital, her doctor came to see me. He said that she had developed a very high fever, but he didn't know why.

He said it was really serious, and he wasn't sure she'd make it. He added that he hoped her things were in order. In other words, prepare for the worst. That was hard to hear, but when in doubt, pray. I asked God for the endurance she needed to get through the ordeal. Not only my family and I, but many friends all over the country sought God's intervention that day.

With her barely hanging on, it took several days for the doctors to figure out the cause. Finally, the lab workers discovered the infection, which led to the right treatment. The question was whether or not the infection could be stopped in time.

Praise God, our prayers were answered. Her fever abated quickly after the treatment took effect, and Donna survived. However, I was told that even though the treatment worked, she shouldn't have survived. She had been at too high a fever level for way too long.

When I thanked the doctor, he said, "Don't thank me, John. I didn't do anything to save her. I expected her to leave us. In fact, I can't practically explain what kept her alive. She lived much longer than she should have with that high of a fever. It's a God story, son!"

And so it was; another miracle had happened. Praise our eternal God!

"Consider it all joy, my brethren, when you encounter various trials, knowing that the testing of your faith produces endurance." (James 1:2-3 NASB)

CHAPTER 14

My Lifesaving Surprise

In the fall of 1988, a truly unexpected surprise happened. I was still a church bond broker but also worked as a director of development with a Christian academy in Western Pennsylvania. One morning, after an administrative staff meeting, June, the elementary principal, asked to see me in her office. She said she had questions about the capital campaign we were planning. However, there was one other thing she wanted to discuss with me. She said it had nothing to do with work, which intrigued me. It turned out to be even more startling than I thought.

She began the conversation with, "My mother thinks we are related." When I asked what her maiden name was, she replied, "Hays." I quickly said, "Oh! My sister, Janice, married Raphael Hays from Carlisle, PA . . ."

Before I could go on, June said, "No, she thinks your father was her favorite cousin. Did they ever call him 'Pige' [pronounced Pidge]?" I didn't like his nickname but acknowledged that they did. Apparently, my father, John W. Corfield, Sr., as a youngster would "flit" around like a pigeon. His friends were the ones to give him that nickname, and after a while, it was shortened to Pige. Dad's nickname was also confirmed the following summer on a golf course in the North Hills. A man from the foursome behind me yelled, "I heard your name, John Corfield, when you were called to proceed to the first tee. Was your father's nickname Pige?"

It turned out that this old gentleman had gone to Allegheny High School with my dad. Apparently, Pige had been a very popular guy, which seemed to line up well with his character.

Getting back to the meeting with the principal, it hit me that I was actually sitting in front my second cousin June. It's possible we may have met when I was very young, but I don't remember it. Once we had established that we were indeed cousins, June invited my wife and me to dinner. She wanted us to meet her mother, Jesse. The invitation was gladly accepted.

The Lord had set up another divine appointment. It was not only a great time to meet new family, but also to learn something very important, so important it literally saved my life!

As we were invited to enter their home, my eighty-four-year-old cousin Jesse said, "I know you, John Weller!" I realized she was seeing my father, whom I had begun to resemble in those days. Today, I look even more like him. In fact, there was a definite time when that became obvious. While shaving one morning, I felt as if there was someone else behind me. I turned to ask, "Dad, what are you doing here?" That wasn't Dad in the mirror, it was I. Where had John, Jr., gone? I couldn't believe it. It hadn't occurred to me that Jesse would immediately see the resemblance. As far as looks go, I am Dad, and will be for the rest of my life. I'm actually happy about that.

We learned a lot about the Corfield side of the family that night at diner. I hadn't known much about them growing up. My mother didn't appreciate a comment about her weight, which was the beginning of a frosty relationship with the Corfield side.

It also didn't help that Mom didn't drive, which meant we didn't visit anyone very often. We even had a cousin, Karen, in the borough just south of ours, but I only met her once. Mom gave me something to deliver to her mother. However, the overwhelming effort needed to keep our big old DeSoto from sliding off the icy road was my major concern. It's probable that not much more than hello was said. I just wanted to get that car back home safely. However, knowing Karen as I do now, that was a big mistake.

Today, Karen and I are great friends. We often communicate through email. Both of us teach adult Sunday-school classes and like to exchange Bible research in preparation for teaching. She is a very strong believer. That may appear to be a Corfield trait.

I had briefly met some Corfield aunts. I told June that I liked Aunt Nellie but wasn't sure why. She said that Aunt Nellie had prayed all of us into the Kingdom. When I asked for more about that, Jesse nodded and then began to tell me about our heritage.

My great grandfather, William Corfield, had brought his family over to America from England sometime around 1880. He and his wife had nine children, but one had passed away. Of the eight remaining children were four boys and four girls.

One of them was my grandfather, John Edward Corfield, but I never met him. He died when I was only four months old. He had seen a picture of me soon after my birth, but that was all. I also have his picture. He looked surprisingly like President Woodrow Wilson. I doubt he'd like that comparison; all of the Corfields were staunch Republicans. Yet, he could have been his twin.

Jesse had a lot of material on the family, including a letter from my great grandfather to his wife back in England. He wrote it while at sea on his way to America. Jesse gave me a copy of the letter, which contains the details of his voyage. As I read it, I could feel his excitement and anticipation for what the Lord had planned for him in the New World. His love for the Lord was just as apparent. What a blessing! But that led me to ask if Dad was a born-again believer.

During my high school days, Dad was asked to be a deacon at our church. Prior to that, he hadn't regularly attended church. Therefore, I'm sure he was surprised when they recruited him for that post. Being a deacon also meant that he had to teach Sunday school, which he took very seriously. My mother told me that he wanted his students to understand who Jesus really was. I wondered how he knew so much about Jesus.

While reading a story from the book of Luke to his students one Sunday morning, he explained that those in the Lord's hometown did not believe that Jesus was the Messiah. Even though they had heard about his miracles, healings, etc., they knew him only as the carpenter's son. Dad asked the class to picture someone they knew in Ben Avon who would suddenly start telling everyone that he was God's Son. He asked one of the boys, "What would you think if someone told you that?" The youngster quickly replied, "I don't know, I don't live in Ben Avon." Dad had a great sense of humor and got a big kick out of that.

Because of his business travel, Dad would occasionally ask me to substitute for him. At the time, I didn't have any real teaching experience, but his specific lesson plans were easy to follow. His questions for the students proved that Dad was not an average teacher; he knew a lot about the Bible. That answered my question as to how he knew so much about Jesus.

Mom hadn't related the boy's story until after I'd become a born-again believer. Still, I wanted to be sure that Dad was really saved. I asked Mom if she thought Dad was a true believer. She said, "You know he was, as were all of the Corfields. In fact, his dad, your grandfather, John Edward, was very outspoken about his faith. He traveled to different churches in Illinois to raise money for Moody Bible Institute."

That said a lot about his dad, but we aren't grandfathered into the Kingdom. We are responsible to receive the Lord individually. I wanted something more definite, which Jesse provided at dinner.

It was obvious from the way Jesse talked about him that she knew him very well. To me, that was an open door to ask if she knew whether or not Dad had ever received Jesus as his personal Savior and Lord. Jesse happily replied, "Oh Yes! He received Christ on the same day I did. He was a very strong believer."

That made all of us at the table very happy, but it also made me wonder why I didn't know that growing up. My mom couldn't have explained it and my dad, who could have, didn't. Perhaps, in those days, people left salvation up to our ministers and teachers.

Dad may have thought I had received Christ. He was there when I had joined our church. To him, perhaps it meant his son was a Christian. I may have even thought so myself. After all, I did pray.

However, being a church member doesn't make one a Christian. That's why, after my salvation experience, I began to wonder whether my parents were saved. I already knew my mom had finally accepted the Lord at the play in Deltona, but Jesse was certain that Dad was a believer.

After that night, this worry never came to me again. We will, one day soon, be reunited in heaven. My wife and I were really happy we went. We were very pleased to have Dad's place in heaven confirmed.

One must ask, though, "What are the odds of going to work at a school where the elementary principal was a cousin of mine that I didn't know?" And from that, I learned how serious the vascular problems on my dad's side were. The medical history came in handy later on.

A great feeling had come from this wonderful evening, but also an omen. What Jesse said concerning the medical history that night would lead to my lifesaving surprise!

"But may the God of all grace, who called us to His eternal glory by Christ Jesus, after you have suffered a while, perfect, establish, strengthen, and settle you." (1 Peter 5:10)

CHAPTER 15

My Wake-Up Call

In January of 1989, I was diagnosed with renal cell carcinoma, a rare form of kidney cancer. Only those who have come down with cancer know the terrible feeling that accompanies hearing the diagnosis for the first time. If I hadn't taken the job with the academy, I may have gone on for years not knowing what was growing inside of me. The Lord not only knew this, but He did another amazing miracle in the way it was discovered.

I told Jessie, "My dad endured an eight-hour operation to repair an aneurism on his aorta below the stomach. That artery had to be replaced by a plastic one that would 'Y' into both legs. It saved his life, but only for the next four years when his life was cut short by lung cancer."

Jesse looked sadly at me and said, "I really miss him. However, you should know that I had that same operation, and there have been four others in the family since mine." About a year after that, she informed me that her sister had just survived the same operation. That made seven family members, counting my dad, with the same condition and procedure.

That startling information made me think about our family medical history that night. Perhaps, it should be checked out. My wife was thinking the same thing. On the way home, she said, "You have a physical this Thursday. Tell the doctor about your family history." I told her that I felt great, but just to be certain nothing was wrong, I would definitely explain it to him. Saying that I'm really glad I did is an understatement!

My doctor thought for several seconds and said, "It's expensive, but we should keep an eye on it in case you do have an aneurism. We need to do an ultrasound." I didn't expect the procedure to find what it did, but I should have realized something was wrong. The technician took only about five minutes on my left side, but twenty minutes or more on the right side.

Two weeks later, my doctor called to tell me that he had good news and bad news. "The good news is that your arterial system is fine." I asked, "What about the bad news?" He said, "There is something on top of your right kidney." I asked if it was a cyst. He replied, "No, we know that for certain." Then he said that he wouldn't be able to tell what it is without more tests. That was a shock, to say the least. I owe what happened next, in part, to the late Dr. Peter Marshall.

As I hung up the phone, a cold chill came over me. I asked the Lord for help, and He provided it. Right there on my desk was a book called *The Messages of Peter Marshall*, about whom the book *A Man Called Peter* was written. After his death, *A Man Called Peter*, written by his wife, Kathrine Marshall, was made into a movie.

It was a tear-jerking movie. I saw it with a friend and his family when we were in sixth grade. I also saw it again with a girlfriend in ninth grade. It was a reward for selling more than twenty dollars worth of magazines. She loved that movie because, as she said, "He was a man of faith." Peter Marshall also spent the last two years of his life as the chaplain of the U.S. Senate. A sudden heart attack took his life in 1949 at the age of forty-seven.

While pondering, my thumb fanned the pages. I don't even know why that book was in my hand, but I opened to read, *"The man of God does not worry about the worst thing that could happen to him. He should trust God and be thankful for every day that he lives."*

Suddenly, the peace that passes all understanding came over me like a flood. I knew I would get through it. Of course, sharing the results with my arthritic wife wouldn't be easy. She was always the one in the hospital bed, and I was the one in the chair. It was not to be this time.

Over 95 percent of kidney tumors are malignant, mine was no exception.

For some reason, my arterial system had an irregularity with regard to my right kidney. There were two major arteries going into that kidney instead of one. The main artery was serving the kidney itself, without it being affected in any way by the tumor. For that reason, the kidney was working perfectly.

However, the other artery was feeding the tumor, which was sitting on top of the kidney. I watched it on a monitor after a camera was maneuvered through an artery to the kidney. As the tech said, he was creating a road map for the operation. Until this incident, I had never had anything greater than a treadmill test. This test was my least favorite of any prior to or after my kidney operation. Where that second artery came from didn't matter. Protocol was to remove the kidney and then check the tumor, which was found to be malignant.

Renal cell carcinoma is very slow growing, and I was in stage 1A, which couldn't have been better. The tumor was encapsulated, meaning that a callus had formed over it. Upon examination of the encapsulation, no cancer cells were found within it. My urologist told me afterward that it would have taken six years to feel the pain. However, by then, it may have been too late. I had dodged a bullet for certain. It was through June and Jesse, that the Lord made it happen.

I have survived twenty-nine years now, with no problem in the other kidney. The entire process of discovering it and getting it out early was miraculous. What are the odds that I would be hired by a school where a cousin of mine whom I didn't know would be responsible, along with her mother, for saving my life? I thank God that my cousin June discovered our connection and invited us to dinner. I thank God for Jesse, who related the family medical history to me, which would come in handy later for another incredible reason.

A miracle is not just for the one who experiences it, but also for others. A family blessing occurred from this experience. The night I met my cousin Jessie, she also told me that she really liked my mom. She said she always felt bad that my grandmother, Mama, had preferred another relative over her. I thought Mom would like to know how Jesse felt, and I was right. After telling her what Jesse had said, Mom quickly wrote a letter to her. The two of them were great friends for many years after that. They kept in touch until Jesse passed.

At the age of ninety-four, Jesse went to be with the Lord. I miss her but will see her again. Meeting and getting to know June and Jesse was a real gift of joy. It reinforced how the Lord does provide for our special needs, some of which we may be unaware. I would have continued to be unaware of my problem if it hadn't been for that evening.

God used them in the miracle of saving my life by the eradication of a very serious medical condition. I am very grateful to Him for my wakeup call.

"And all these blessings shall come upon you and overtake you . . ."
(Deuteronomy 28:2 NKJV)

Chapter 16

Difficult Times

My wife's condition had gone south sometime after getting to know June and Jesse. I was beginning to experience difficulty in the parts of a development director's job that I didn't know. Let me state that no one wakes up in the morning wanting to be a fundraiser. I was no different. However, it was very enjoyable once it turned out not to be what I envisioned. Determining what was necessary to succeed in major capital fundraising was hard at first, but it finally came together.

In 1992, I started my own Christian School Capital Fundraising business. I loved my new career. However, in 1995, I had to take a number of years off from my business for my wife's sake. As her condition worsened, a more permanent position with less travel was needed to keep me close to home.

It was obvious to me that Donna wanted to move back to California to be closer to her parents, which was understandable. I not only agreed but encouraged the idea. It wasn't because of my desire to move back there. Pittsburgh is my beloved hometown, and the southwest part of Pennsylvania is where my heart is. However, when her doctors started hinting that she didn't have a lot of time left, the decision was easy.

Once settled back in California, I went to work for a Christian college as one of two development directors. That was the first of three Christian colleges or universities where I served in that capacity. In less than two years, however, I had to leave the college because of a medical emergency. My wife had aspirated after an MRI, and it changed everything. She lost much of her memory, due to the time it took to resuscitate her. That she was able to be resuscitated was a miracle in itself, but this time, there were consequences.

She fell back into a coma for over a week. Sometimes, she would come halfway out of it. However, it was clear that she had lost much of her memory. She recognized her mother, probably because she still looked much like she did in her younger years. However, she did not recognize her father at first. Donna was much more in than out of the coma for the next few days.

Our son Troy came to see her when it looked as if she wasn't going to come out of it. Both of us were standing over her bed, when Troy said, "Wake up, Mom." Suddenly, her eyes opened as if surprised. She looked up at me and immediately said my name and grabbed my hand. Looking a little confused, she said, "Where do we live?" I said, "We live in Newhall." That she seemed to remember was a good sign. I hoped things were returning to normal until she asked me for a mirror. She didn't recognize the image she saw in it. That said everything.

My job after that was to help her get her memory back. There was no way I could stay at the college and do that. My superiors were of the same opinion. Her condition and corresponding hospital stays took too much of my attention. It was difficult to concentrate on my work. But, they kindly waited for me to bring up the fact that it was time to leave. They gave me a three months' severance, which was meted out over five months. I am very grateful for their kindness.

Donna recovered about half of her memory through our many discussions. I could tell when she would remember things because she would add personal facts that went with the memories. It was also obvious when she wasn't getting it. She would only smile and nod. That was very difficult for both of us. The fact that she lived through it all for another year and a half was a real blessing and a miracle.

When I finally had to go back to work, the president of another Christian college contacted me. I was hired to be the director of development, major donors and capital campaigns.

That was a lot to put on my business card. Good things happened in the three years I was there. I had conducted a feasibility study with them, which told me only four of the board members were giving to the college. All but four of the thirty-plus member board began to donate after that.

We initiated a successful campaign to become a university, and eventually built a new Business and Theology building. Unfortunately, before that building was built, I had to leave with several other high-paid employees. A young auditor wrote that we hadn't been reporting the depreciation of our buildings properly. It threatened the closure of the university. Fortunately, that didn't happen and things returned to normal. However, by that time, another university had hired me to be the director of development (DOD) for their renown School of Theology.

Through it all, I learned a lot about a DOD's role, including how to successfully cultivate donors, especially major ones. What success I experienced in capital fundraising was the Lord's. However, there were also failures, which were mine. I learned a lot from both success and failure, as is normal in Christian life. The training the Lord gave me while working on the inside with college constituent donors and other groups afterward was a great education.

In 2005, I restarted Corfield Consulting Services. I had realized something. All of my accumulated fundraising experience could help to mentor Christian school DODs. Meeting and successfully cultivating major donors made that possible. The beauty of it is the DOD makes a lot of great friends in the process. Having experience in both outside and inside capital fundraising became invaluable to me in my consulting business.

Overall, I have really enjoyed my fundraising career and experience, although some of it happened during very difficult family times.

"For I have learned in whatever state I am, to be content:"
(Philippians 4:11 NKJV)

CHAPTER 17

Saying Goodbye

Donna, my wife of twenty-five years, passed away in May of 1998. During her eighteen-year battle with severe rheumatoid arthritis, I used the same phrase that just came out when praying for my friend Ron. I laid hands on my wife and prayed, "Be healed in the name of the Lord Jesus Christ." I did that many times, but to no avail. Again, no one today has the gift of healing, and there is no formula that works every time. The reason for that is the sovereignty of God. It is the Lord who does the healing, not the vessel He uses. And, He decides when and whom He heals, the vessel is just the conduit of His works.

It's said that rheumatoid arthritis doesn't kill anyone. That may be technically true, but its medications often create conditions that can. Cancer doesn't kill anyone either, pneumonia does, but we all know that cancer weakens the organs and the body first. Once they start shutting down, the pneumonia follows.

In the case of arthritis, high amounts of steroids are great at masking the pain, but prolonged use devastates the joints, muscles, tendons, and bones. Osteoporosis, a weakening of the bones, is the worst. Donna's osteoporosis was so severe she lost nine inches in height. Her bones were so weak that they began to break almost for no reason. Her tendons were also affected. She had a shoulder surgery to repair a painful tendon in her left shoulder, but it only lasted a few days before the repaired tendon snapped. It was hard to watch.

Through all of the pain and sorrow, the Lord was implementing His plan for Donna. If she had been healed, there may have been no one to witness the love of Christ to the many medical professionals. They were always confounded by her love for God. The Lord used Donna's many hospital stays to naturally witness to those in the medical profession, especially the nurses.

She wasn't one to quote Bible verses, tracts, or the "Four Spiritual Laws." She would just relate the great things the Lord had done for her and how she knew Him as her best friend. She trusted God for everything. She suffered more than anyone I had ever known over an eighteen-year period, yet, she did not blame God. She believed He knew what He was doing. As she put it, "God doesn't make mistakes."

In the minds of those that treated her, she should have been shaking her fist at God for all of the terrible conditions and operations God allowed her to endure, but she never did.

She had a God-given gift of helps that she used all of her life. Of course, when Donna felt trapped in her own body because of her condition, she became deeply saddened. In her mind, her gift of helps could no longer be used to minister to others, but she still never blamed God.

In actuality, she did use her gift of helps and in a way that really touched the nurses. During one hospital stay, I decided to visit her before going to work. When I arrived at the nurses' station, two of them were crying. That was not a good sign.

At first, I had thought Donna had passed away. Fearing that possibility, I asked if anything serious had happened to her. They assured me that nothing medically happened with her, it was her love for God. They had never before witnessed anyone having such great faith. They felt she should have been furious with God. Instead, she continued to love and trust Him.

They didn't know it was for their benefit. I doubt if Donna knew it either. They were seeing the love of Christ through the life of a true but suffering believer.

First Timothy 1:16 tells us that believers may experience long suffering. This is to turn them to depend on Christ for everything. Ultimately, it is that love for God which others saw in her.

That, in itself, glorifies God. It is His witness of an eternal life in Him by faith alone, no matter what may be happening to the sufferer.

Upon hearing she was still with us, I was relieved. But, in going on to explain that we were both born-again Christians, they looked at me and said, "We don't know about you." Ouch!

In perceiving me to be overly attentive to her treatment, they were not seeing Christ in me. To remain steadfast in watching that Donna was handled correctly, I had little choice. However, I began to do it in a nicer way after that comment. Whether it worked or not, I don't know, but it seemed to cut down on confrontations.

However, whoever took her for an MRI totally ignored her chart. After being returned asleep from an MRI, they didn't wake Donna up to place her on the bed. Instead, they just placed her carefully into bed, but on her back. The doctor had stipulated that no one was to ever do that, but they didn't know it. They hadn't read her chart.

Her new roommate didn't know anything about that prohibition either. Therefore, when it happened, no one was there to correct the problem. Whatever the reason, she was left in that dangerous position, from which she barely survived. Donna slept that way long enough to aspirate. As a result, my wife nearly died from the choking. That was a terrible experience, which caused a huge loss of memory.

Instead of going straight to the hospital from work that day, I had decided to have dinner at a restaurant first. It was Friday, and I was very tired. Once I finally entered her hospital room, she wasn't there. Her roommate then told me what happened. She said they took her to the emergency room. I ran as fast as I could to the ER—only to see Donna lying on a gurney, out in the open, with a ventilator stuck in her mouth. I thought she was dead, but she wasn't.

That one mistake seriously impaired Donna's chances of ever recovering from her conditions. Besides that, all the medicines that helped her deal with the pain actually made her conditions worse. She passed away a little over a year after that incident.

The final sad moment came several days before we had closed on a home in Laguna Hills. She never got the chance to reside there.

Donna was wheelchair bound for much of her last days. She could get around the house with a walker, but when I had to leave for work, the wheelchair was generally used. As her condition worsened, she found it hard to use either one.

I ordered an electric wheelchair to help her get around more easily. When it arrived, I was really excited for her and couldn't wait for her to try it. Unfortunately, she was too tired. She was also having hallucinations from the new upgraded morphine dosage.

The next day, she was gone. It was hard to grasp, but as she said, the Lord doesn't make mistakes. She'd always said she felt trapped in a body that wouldn't let her do what she wanted. Though the thought that she was truly free with the Lord was comforting, it didn't make her loss any easier for me or our family.

Seeing the smile on her face as she passed away made me believe that she was actually seeing Jesus. I hadn't seen her in such a tranquil state for a very long time. Although I went into panic mode at that point, looking back on it now, I am grateful to the Lord for her smile.

If I am right, she was looking at the Lord Jesus. God loves His created servants more than I or anyone else on earth ever could.

Saying goodbye to someone you love is never easy. It was a very sad moment for me. However, it seemed, from her smile, to be an eternal relief for her. It can't be proven, but as that last breath left her, I believe her smile served to assure me that she went happily with the Lord.

"To be absent from the body is to be present with the Lord."
(2 Corinthians 5:8 NKJV)

Chapter 18

In Transition

The transition, which is never easy, was made somewhat easier through my colleagues, church, and family. I feel very blessed to have had the support I needed. The president of the university was a huge help. He came to see me the night of her passing to go over what needed to be done. He took care of all the funeral arrangements and even performed the ceremony.

The next day, friends from the university, along with the majority of our adult Sunday-school class, stopped by to see me. It was good to have friends help me through it, especially with the things I wasn't ready to handle. With all of the issues that nearly took her life throughout the years, I should have been ready when it finally happened, but I wasn't. No one is ever ready to lose a spouse!

I didn't want to face any of it. In fact, it was very hard to sleep the first night. Although I had plenty of warnings that her time on earth was coming to a close, it took me over four months not to weep a little when talking about her passing. Therefore, I tried to avoid it.

It was finally over, and she was free. However, suddenly there was no longer anyone in this life totally dependent on me. Of course, that is a mischaracterization; she depended on God to work through me. Through it all, I had come to realize what caregiving truly is. Although it definitely isn't easy, in many ways it is a tremendous blessing.

My sister Judy, cousin Cris, our daughter Tracee, and family came from back east for the funeral. They also helped me a lot the following week, especially in getting Donna's things together and the move to the new house. Before she left, Tracee invited me to meet with them in Beulah Beach, Ohio. She also told me that Mom didn't want me to mourn too long, but to go out, meet people, and even date.

The people with whom I worked made things easier. As time went on and I was ready, they encouraged me to date. But actually, it scared me a lot. When one has been married for twenty-five years, it's not as easy as it once was to return to the dating scene.

My first attempt was difficult. The second attempt went better, but neither one was easy. It had nothing to do with the people I dated, they were very nice. It just wasn't comfortable yet. However, one day in church, a woman caught my eye, who, by her kind behavior with her daughter, I thought I would like to meet. I didn't know if the Lord was in agreement with me at the time, but if He was, we would meet. I am very grateful to God for what came next. He definitely led me to complete the transition, whether I thought I was ready or not. I learned the meaning of:

"And my God shall supply all your needs, according to His riches in glory by Christ Jesus." (Philippians: 4:19 NKJV)

CHAPTER 19

My Gift from God

I didn't attend church services much during my wife's last year. I always went to adult Sunday school and then came home to take care of her. After her passing and getting settled afterward, the church service was added to my Sunday-morning worship experience.

When the time came to attend church, I did it gladly. It was definitely needed. One Sunday morning, I noticed the university business manager standing by himself. I walked over to him while everyone was standing to sing. He didn't notice me at first; he seemed distracted by a sign. When asked what he was doing, he replied, "I'm checking the big board."

He pointed to a sign that had a number on it. The big board, as he called it, was no larger than an exit sign. Apparently, if his son acted up in his kindergarten class, a number would alert him to come get his boy. At that moment, his number appeared. With a chuckle, he left.

While pondering the ingenuity of that simple system, my eyes dropped down to a woman and her daughter. Somehow, I could tell the woman really loved her daughter by the way she was talking with her. My prayer was for the Lord to send me someone like her.

He not only did, but I was soon to realize she was the one! On another Sunday morning, I walked into church with the wife of my friend, Jerry, the Southern California regional director for the Association of Christian Schools International (ACSI). He and his wife were good friends of mine, as well as Sunday-school classmates. They were also friends with Sherri, the woman who'd caught my eye.

However, at the time, I didn't know they knew her. To my surprise, Sherri was sitting next to Jerry. I sat down on the other side of him. I asked if he knew her. He said, "Yes. Her name is Sherri. Her two daughters attended college here." When I asked if she was a single mother, Jerry confirmed that she was.

At the invitation of the pastor, many of us went forward to form prayer lines. Once we had formed two long lines, the pastor said to put a hand on someone on our left and pray for that person, which I did. Then he said to put a hand on someone on our right and do the same. There was no one on my right, so I looked in front of me, and there was Sherri. I put my hand on her shoulder and prayed for her.

When she turned around, I introduced myself as the college director of development. She gave me a halfway hug and said, "I'm sorry to hear about your wife." She then walked back to her seat.

I was surprised that she knew of my wife's passing. The chapel had been full at the memorial service, but I didn't see Sherri there. She hadn't been there, but a friend of hers had. When I returned to my seat, I asked Jerry how she knew about my wife. He said that she probably heard it from her best friend, a classmate of ours. He mentioned her friend's name, but I didn't recognize it. I've always been terrible with names, which is not a good trait for a director of development.

It took me two weeks to ask Sherri out, but once it happened, I was sold. I met her after church and talked with her for a while. She was not only a fine mother, but she also visited her aunt in Long Beach every Sunday. In fact, when I asked her to have lunch with me, she turned me down. At first, I thought she wasn't interested, but then she told me that she had to visit her aunt but would be glad to meet me at the church later to go out for dinner. That's what I wanted to hear! Sherri confessed that evening of having no idea what a director of development does. Most people don't. I just laughed. It was a wonderful evening.

Seven months later, we were married. We recently celebrated our nineteenth anniversary. Sherri has been a big help to me in my fundraising and expanded ministry. I will always be grateful for—my gift from God.

> *"Every good gift and every perfect gift is from above, and comes down from the Father of lights, with whom there is no variation or shadow of turning"* (James 1:17 NKJV)

CHAPTER 20

Love Thy Neighbor

I left my college fundraising career for three years to work for a media watchdog group. It was a great experience. However, I came to the conclusion that my trust must be in God only, not the government. There are problems in both parties that have been hurting our nation. God raises up all leaders, which many Christians believe coincides with fulfilled prophecy. Whoever we have at any time is from Him for His reasons, whether we understand or not. That is true of every age and every nation.

Working with that organization was interesting, but my true calling was working with Christian ministries, especially Christian day schools. However, I am grateful to the watchdog organization in what I learned about major donors who were not necessarily Christian. That experience would help later in various ways.

It took us a while to sell our house in Southern California and move to Northern Virginia. Once we did, we bought a great house in the Cascades area of Sterling. One day, while working at home, a lifesaving miracle happened. There were alerts that tornados may occur in Maryland and our area that day. We lived right across the Potomac from Maryland.

There was a downpour for a few minutes accompanied by very strong winds. It stirred me to walk into our bedroom. I wanted to see what was going on in the backyard.

We had a very tall oak tree on the border of our backyard. Directly across from our three-bedroom windows was the tree's largest branch. A mini burst cleanly sliced off the huge branch just as I opened the blinds. As it headed in my direction, there was no time for me to react. If it had hit the window, I would have bought the farm.

Because the wind was swirling, it directed the branch toward our house, but thankfully downward, as would a wind shear. That actually saved my life! Instead of hitting our windows upstairs, the heavy branch hit the deck below. With a loud smack, it created a huge hole in the deck, which saved the four family-room windows. The trunk stuck firmly in the hole, which allowed its smaller branches to only brush up against the windows. That was a Godsend!

To put its size in perspective, it stretched almost from one end of our colonial house to the other end and about halfway into the side yard of our neighbor's home. Since the branch blocked the sliding glass door, the garage was the best exit. Our new neighbor to be was standing there as I walked out to inspect the damage. I invited her to see it. While approaching the rear of the house, we saw the end of the branch lying partially in her new side yard.

She didn't seem bothered by it, just amazed. Another big branch was left hanging on the tree. It had to be removed, along with the bigger branch on the deck. Amazingly, it had been completely taken care of within twenty-four hours of the incident.

At the time of this incident, Sherri was back in California. The next day, I was back at my work. When I returned home that evening, the branches had been removed. However, in returning home the next day, I couldn't understand how the hole in the deck was repaired.

Our original neighbor saw me drive up. She told me her father fixed the deck for us. He came all the way from Richmond and had already started back. That's about a six-hour round trip. Apparently, Sherri had talked with the neighbor. I didn't even get a chance to thank him. God had saved my life again, and my neighbor had helped us out, saving us time. I will never forget their kindness. I think of them whenever I read *love thy neighbor.*

"And a second is like the first, love thy neighbor as thyself."
(Matthew: 22:39 NKJV)

CHAPTER 21

Three Road Lifesavers

I'm going to switch gears (no pun intended) to several miracles that I experienced while driving. One occurred before I was saved and three afterward. All of them were lifesavers, which makes me believe that the Lord protects us always, even when we have walked away from Him to follow the things of the world. If He has work for us to do, He will keep us here. I'm the proof of that. Here are the first three road lifesaving events for which I credit the Lord.

I had a driving experience in which my foot responded to danger before I even thought about it. After my college graduation, I went to Illinois to help my sister and brother-in-law with a marital problem. My three nieces were a lot of fun to be around, and I liked that. My spending more time with the nieces gave my sister and her husband time to work out their problem. A cousin of mine also lived in the area at that time, which was also a plus.

Once settled in, I got a temporary job at a hotel, something I had done my last year in college. While driving to work through a rural area before sunrise one day, there was a railroad crossing that I didn't see. It was very dark that morning. The two-lane road crossed a single railroad track with no gates or warning lights. As I approached the crossover, my peripheral vision noticed a light that appeared to be stationary. I should have known better. I was in farm country where there weren't many streets, let alone lights.

My foot suddenly stomped on the brake, just in time to stop my car from being hit by a train. I had to sit there for what seemed like

91

an eternity as the train's cars went by slowly in front of me, probably no more than a yard or so away. Fortunately, the train passed without hitting my car. After it was gone, I realized my foot was still firmly on the brake. I was so shocked by the reaction and seeing the train as it passed in front of me, I hadn't even put the car in park. However, that was a good thing; it kept the car from rolling forward. The Lord had stepped in, even if I hadn't realized it.

My cousin, upon hearing the story, said, "Be careful, people die that way around here." What made my foot react in that way prior to my realizing the danger? Since I hadn't felt any fear, it had to have been divine intervention. The fear didn't set in until after the event was over. But I didn't worry about it; after all, I was still alive. I didn't give God the credit, but I should have.

The second lifesaving experience came during my time as a Christian-school-curriculum representative. This time, my hands were involved instead of my feet. In my third year with the company, we transferred from California to the Illinois territory. This miracle, in what should have been a terrifying experience, happened while driving north to return home. Route 51 was a two-lane road that split the state from north to south. It was spring, and we were in a driving rainstorm, which slowed the trucks coming in the opposite direction. It was really hard to see, but I was intent on getting home. In retrospect, I should have pulled off the road long before it got that bad.

Suddenly, a white car pulled out from behind an approaching truck, and it was right in front of me. I said softly and calmly, "Lord, here I come." At that moment, something made my hands turn the wheel to the right but only slightly. It was enough of a turn to create a narrow space between the truck and my car. Miraculously, the other driver was able to barely get through. All I saw with my peripheral vision was a white blur flying between the truck and me. But that wasn't the end of it.

The next thing I knew, I hit the berm on the right side of the road, which threw my car across the road to the other side. Once on that berm, my car was thrown back again to the right side. My car finally slid to a stop just outside the edge of a bridge.

That was a good thing. A few more feet and I would have gone over the embankment and into the creek below. While sitting there looking at the water for about five minutes, I thanked God for whatever He just did. I had been expecting to talk with Him face-to-face, not still sitting in my undamaged car. That our cars didn't hit head on was definitely a miracle, especially since the other driver was accelerating.

The average person would have instinctively hit the brakes and made a hard turn, which may have rolled my car. Thankfully, I didn't have time to react. The Lord did it in His way for me, as He has at other times. What happened had nothing to do with me. Of this, I am positive.

Considering the fact that no cars were behind me or the white car was also a miracle. My car would have hit another car or two on both drivers' sides. That could have brought about a fatal end result, which I was expecting to happen with the white car.

Before backing up to re-enter the road, I looked in my rearview mirror. I saw the white car parked on the other side of the road. He or she was either waiting to see if I was okay or thanking God as I was. Once I started across the bridge, the white car pulled out and continued south.

The third incident was a similar miracle to the second. It occurred after our transfer to the Pennsylvania territory, which I had hoped to get since my hiring. When that opportunity came, we moved to Elizabethtown, Pennsylvania. We were only there a few weeks before the next event happened.

It was almost exactly the same scenario as the Illinois incident, but with different weather conditions. It was a clear and fairly warm evening. We were returning home from a church service, and we were very tired. My wife Donna saw something that I didn't. Suddenly, she screamed, "That car is on our side of the road!" Before I thought about it, my hands performed the exact same maneuver as it did the last time. However, because there was no storm and there was a paved berm, we came to a complete stop without a problem as the other car sped past, just missing us.

My wife said to our son Troy and me, "If he had hit us, the three of us would have been killed and our daughter Tracee would not have known what happened." Tracee was visiting a new friend that night. Her friend's parents would have returned her to a dark and empty house.

In the rearview mirror, I could see the car continuing down the wrong side of the road. The next day, I purchased a newspaper, expecting to read about a fatal accident on that road the previous night. Thankfully, what I feared had not happened. Again, for me, it was a great example of—***the protection of the Lord***.

"For You have been a shelter for me." (Psalm 61:3 NKJV)

CHAPTER 22

Our Miracle Car

The last road miracle happened the year we moved to Arizona. We were on our way to visit a good friend in Fountain Hills, Arizona. Sherri wanted to drive that morning, which I appreciated. I was tired. As we entered the freeway, she mentioned that she wished we could get a new car. I said, "We aren't buying a new car until the Lord shows us that we really need one."

About a half hour later, we exited the freeway. We continued to our friend's home without any problem until we came to our friend's road. Having first slowed enough to make a sharp right turn, the entire front left side of the car dropped. Because of the turn, it had wedged on top of the left front tire. Otherwise, Sherri could not have exited the car.

We both quickly looked to see that there weren't any gas or oil leaks. After assessing that there weren't any, I started to laugh out loud. My wife, still in shock, asked, "What are you laughing about?" Excitedly, I replied, "The Lord just told us to buy a new car!"

If it had happened while we were traveling on the freeway, either to or from our friend's home, we would have been strewn all over the road. The car held up just long enough for us to almost get there, which made it a miracle. Having it happen just prior to arriving at our destination prevented us from leaving later with a very serious problem.

Our friend called a tow company and had them deliver the car to her mechanic. The ball joint had broken in half. The mechanic said it was the first of our car's brand he'd ever seen do that. Our model, he thought, was one of the most reliable cars on the road. I had only once heard of that happening to any car, and that was fifty years ago. Although our friend's mechanic repaired it really well, we knew we wouldn't have it long.

We stayed over that evening and picked up the car the next morning. We drove straight to a dealership to buy a new bottom-of-the-line full-sized model, at least that's what we thought. It never occurred to us that it was the last day of the month. Dealers have to clear their inventory on that day. Therefore, they offer very good deals to get rid of them.

We were shown a middle-of-the-line car, which had all sorts of new technology. We said we couldn't afford it, but they showed us how we could. They gave us three thousand dollars more for our trade-in than the eight thousand high blue book value, which I knew beforehand. And they lowered the price of the new one considerably.

It's a wonderful car, and it gets great gas mileage. Once again, the Lord provided a lifesaving miracle. We thanked Him, as always, for that. The car is now referred to as—our miracle car.

"Declare His glory among the nations, His wonders among all peoples."
(1 Chronicles 16:24 NKJV)

CHAPTER 23

"Lord, Is It Time to Come Home?"

This miracle was another wake-up call for me. But before explaining it, credit must be given to my wife, Sherri, for trying to keep me healthy over the past eighteen years. After this miracle, I seriously jumped in line with her program. It had to be done.

Sherri sees to it that I take vitamins and eat a balanced diet every day. Zetia and red yeast rice are also taken to control cholesterol. The combination of the latter lowered my cholesterol one hundred points over a year. For the first time in my adult life, I am below two hundred. My cholesterol test after taking the combination was 160. I have been the beneficiary of her efforts.

A few years ago, I generally averaged a daily weight of about 212–215 pounds. Being that I am over six feet tall, I had always considered that to be a comfortable weight for me. Biscuits and gravy combo every Tuesday morning with my friends from church was my pig-out meal. I was able to keep my weight down the rest of the week. Therefore, I was fine with my diet, but there was a problem. My blood sugar level had spiked. An annual blood test for my physical two years from this writing put me at ninety-nine; one point under the prediabetic level.

At the request of my doctor, I had another blood test in ninety days, which he compared to my first one. There was another spike in the blood sugar. It showed that my blood sugar level had moved into the prediabetic stage by seven points to 106. One of my friends said that a prediabetic person is a diabetic in training. That hit me hard.

Diabetes is part of our family medical history. Two of my mother's family members had problems with it. And, more recently, one of my sons had a stomach bypass to lose enough weight to better deal with it. He has lost over one hundred pounds since the operation. I'm proud of him for it, but I don't want that for me. Therefore, I looked at what my eating habits were to bring it up to that level. It didn't take long to figure out what I was having between meals.

I had been sweet treating myself a lot more than I realized. Therefore, it was important for me to cut down on the sugar. Gone are the chai tea lattes I was making for myself almost every day. I always drink unsweetened ice tea during the day anyway. But, I also cut the occasional chocolate brownies I would buy whenever lattes were ordered. Milk chocolate has been replaced with dark chocolate made from 85 percent cocoa. Just by cutting down on that much sugar over three months had a profound effect. My blood sugar dropped back to eighty-seven. An A1C test done recently was also below the prediabetic stage.

By sticking closely to the healthy diet, I'm down to 195 pounds for a morning weight. I haven't totally given up the biscuits and gravy combo, even though my Bible-study friends love to kid me if I order it. I order it less now, but it's still an enjoyable habit that's hard to break.

What got me to get on the healthy diet bandwagon? It was another great medical miracle, which happened June 6, 2013. It was surviving an emboli attack of my left lung. A pulmonary embolism is a complication arising from deep-vein thrombosis, resulting in a blood clot blocking the pulmonary artery or branches.

In my case, it was an infarction of the lung. Small blood clots, called emboli, traveled through my heart to my left lung only. The clots created scar tissue in my lower left lung, but that was all. Once there, the clots were either ingested or coughed out. It was thought that the emboli attack came from a small clot in my left foot, but that wasn't certain. The problem generally happens when an injury to a leg results in a clot. I don't know when my emboli condition started.

Bumping my left calf on a wrought-iron coffee table could have done it, but that had been too many years earlier. But then, falling down the steps of the Verizon Center in DC and bruising a muscle in my left calf could also have been the culprit. That one was actually rather comical.

We were there to watch an army military show. I couldn't wait to see the US Army drill team again. It had been many years since I had served in that capacity. Before the show started, I decided to get a rare cola. My wife asked me to buy a large one that we could split, which I did.

As I reached the top of the stairs on the way back, the right side was clear but not the left. I transferred my big cola to my right hand and grabbed the handrail with my left and started down. There was no problem until a group of boys came running up on my side. They were looking down and didn't see me. Before they could pass me, I reached a landing and moved over to the left side. By then, it had been vacated. As I started to transfer my drink to my left hand, I had already started down the stairs. Suddenly the stiff heel on my left shoe caught the top step.

The next thing I knew, I was flopping down the steep steps on my left side holding my right arm up with the large cola still in hand. I could hear people screaming about getting sprayed by my drink, but I was more concerned with flipping head over heels down the cement steps. Thankfully, that didn't happen. I stopped flopping, incredibly, when I reached my wife's chair.

With my right hand still up in the air still clutching the half empty cup, I called to Sherri. She wanted to help me up, but I only wanted her to take the cup. I got up on my own. My left calf was a little sore and swollen, but there were no broken bones. By walking up and down a few steps without a problem eliminated that possibility. Of course, the arena safety people wanted to check me out, but I resisted their attempts. I was there to see the drill team and wasn't going to miss that. Therefore, after thanking them, I sat down. I had bruised a muscle, but that was all. Still, it wasn't all that painful, so I stayed put. Thankfully, it never really bothered me again after that.

Watching the drill team brought back many memories. I always felt that we had the best drill in the world, but it had been changed. Nevertheless, I enjoyed the performance. Watching it gave me a feeling of gratitude to the Lord who had allowed me to be a drill team member.

I suppose it's possible that the bruise had spawned the blood clots, which over time moved in small pieces to my foot where they lodged for quite a while. I began to notice swelling in my left foot every now and then. I just assumed that the swelling was from being on my feet for too long; conventions and school board presentations of my program were the reason. Self-diagnosis is never good!

In a three-month period, I had flown all over the country to attend twelve ACSI conventions. That was a lot of planes, not good for my condition. A horrible cough developed during that time, which lasted almost two months. We were residing in Steilacoom, WA, housesitting for one of Sherri's relatives. We hadn't looked for a local doctor because we weren't sure where the Lord was going to send us next. However, I wanted to know what was causing the cough.

A Christian school in central Pennsylvania contacted me to do a feasibility study. They not only needed one, but they needed it done fairly soon. This opportunity gave me a chance to remedy that problem.

First, I flew into Pittsburgh to see my doctor in Wexford, Pennsylvania. The cough couldn't be shaken, and it was getting worse. He thoroughly checked me out but couldn't determine the problem. I also told him about the swelling in my left foot recently. He checked my leg scan done before we left Cranberry Township, Pennsylvania, for Steilacoom, Washington. He looked at that report, and he didn't see any problem. In fact, the technician had said that I had textbook veins. He couldn't find anything wrong with me, which encouraged me after his diagnosis.

After dinner, I went to my hotel and retired early. But that night would be a hard one. My bad cough kept waking me up. The next day was worse.

I wasn't feeling well at all in the morning. My left side really hurt, but I thought it was a result of coughing. Perhaps, it was a pulled rib-cage muscle. After breakfast in the hotel, I set out for my five-hour drive to Lebanon, Pennsylvania. Just prior to getting in the car, I coughed up a bit of blood. I convinced myself that the dry room air during the night probably dried out my sinuses. That some-times happens to me; again, so much for self-diagnosis!

Almost half way to Lebanon, my left side really hurt. I stopped for lunch outside Harrisburg, walked around awhile after lunch, which seemed to ease the pain. That evening, I made the presenta-tion to the client prospect and succeeded in getting the job.

On the way back to Cranberry, I stopped to get some gas, a sandwich, and then call my wife. I told her that it went well and that we got the client. The plan was to drive all the way back to the Warrendale Holiday Inn Express north of Pittsburgh. Sherri pleaded with me to find a hotel somewhere close to my location, but I wasn't willing to do that. All of my clothes were back at the hotel on the other side of the state. I also had a plane ticket home the next day.

On the surface it seemed like a very bad decision, but I'm really glad I held to it. If I had stayed at one of the hotels nearby, I wouldn't be writing this. Anyway, she told me to be careful and to keep in touch with her on the way back. Unfortunately, it would be only twenty minutes before I would call her.

I entered the Pennsylvania turnpike at Carlisle. Just as I was entering a construction zone, a powerful thunderstorm overtook me. When it occurred to me that I was just sipping air, I became anxious. Trying to take a deep breath caused unbearable pain. It wasn't just my side any longer, but my left shoulder and collarbone as well. I assumed then that a heart attack was in progress, but I was locked in until the next exit.

Beside me on the right was a high wall, which meant there was no place to pull off the road. That lasted for almost twenty miles. I tried to slow down, but the trucks, which couldn't see me because of the storm, were bearing down on me. The rain was so dense I don't think they noticed until they were almost on top of me. I had to keep up with the flow of traffic, which was much faster than normal. Skating into the wall seemed to be a real possibility.

I asked the Lord not to let me black out. Taking someone else with me was my big concern. After prayer, I called Sherri, literally to say goodbye. I told her about the heart-attack possibility and the construction zone, which prevented me from pulling off to the side.

I also told her I loved her but had no idea how this would finish. Of course, I asked for her prayer.

She quickly told me to hang up and call 911. She also reminded me that my sister, Janice, lived in Carlisle. Sherri said she would alert her. Since it sounded like a good plan, I called 911. While relating my condition and the outside circumstances, the 911 operator told me to pull over as soon as possible. My hope was to get to the service area and get out and walk, which seemed to work earlier that afternoon. The 911 operator said, "Please don't do that, you may drop dead." She told me the ambulance was on its way and that she would stay with me until they took over. That was as straight as it gets, and I'm grateful.

About a mile from the service area, the construction zone ended, allowing me to pull over. While thanking God that I made it without an accident, the idea of getting out of the car again came to mind. It was still raining but seemed to be letting up. The 911 operator reminded me once more of what might happen if I did. She told me to recline the seat and wait for the ambulance. She was great! Her calmness kept me at ease.

After about ten minutes, a turnpike service truck and a police car arrived, but the ambulance was still five minutes away. I thanked the 911 operator for staying on the phone with me, but that I should be okay. For some reason, I didn't have the fear that accompanies incidents like this. I knew something was seriously wrong but felt confident that the Lord would come to the rescue.

The officer told me to stay in the car until the ambulance arrived. Once it did, the rain abatement made it easier for the EMTs to load me into it and get to work. An EKG, thankfully, did not indicate a heart attack. The EMTs decided to take me to Carlisle Medical Center. I called Sherri to tell her what was happening. She relayed that information to my sister's voice mail.

Meanwhile, my sister had been honored that night for her community service. Janice has always kept herself active in helping others in her community. It's ingrained in her, to the benefit of any town in which she has lived. To be honored was sheer joy to her. When she arrived back home, she was understandably in a great mood, but tired. She quickly got ready for bed. However, as she was about to turn out the light, she remembered to check her voice mail.

The two messages from Sherri, especially the second one, shocked her. "Your brother is going by ambulance to the Carlisle Medical Center's ER. He didn't have a heart attack, but they need to determine what's going on with him." Thank God, Janice received that message.

If she can help, she jumps into action, and this time was no exception. Normally, it wouldn't have been, if it was for a different reason. She absolutely hates to drive at night, especially outside the Carlisle city limits, and I don't blame her. Anyone familiar with central Pennsylvania towns knows the nights outside of town are generally pitch-black. Jan hadn't driven at night for over ten years, but she did that night.

She gave no consideration to her fear after Sherri's message. Instead, she drove through dark and stormy conditions to get to the medical center. She arrived there just after the ambulance did. She met me in my ER room before I was even settled.

I was glad to see her but was in the middle of answering the ER doctor's questions. He had ordered six vials of blood drawn almost immediately. He then put me through a few tests, but he wasn't satisfied that they had shed any light on my condition.

Because he noticed that I had a temperature of 102, he gave me an antibiotic through my IV. When it went back to normal after that, he concluded that I had pneumonia and decided to release me. Thank God for Jan being there.

My dear sister asked, "Shouldn't that have shown up in the six vials you drew when he first entered the ER?" He said, "Maybe we should do a chest X-Ray to be sure." I didn't even have to get out of bed; he did it right there.

After checking the X-Ray, he said he was now fairly sure what was wrong, but he had to do one more thing, a CT scan. Once he checked the scan, he came back to say, "Mr. Corfield, I have very bad news for you." I said, "No you don't. You're the first person who knows what's wrong and can explain it to me." I added, "And I hope you can tell me what to do about it."

He replied, "You don't understand, you have a very serious condition that you may have to take care of the rest of your life. Are you familiar with the word emboli?" I figured it must be the plural of a blood clot. Therefore, I asked him if it was. He replied, "Yes, you have had pieces of a clot travel through your heart and attack your left lung." That's when he said, "It's called an infarction of the lung."

He went on to say, "When I reviewed the results of your X-Ray and scan, I was expecting to see cloudiness in both lungs. However, it was just a little cloud only at the bottom of the left lung. I realized then what it was." He finished with this warning, "You aren't out of the woods yet, John. I've admitted you to the hospital."

Without thinking, I mentioned going back to Pittsburgh the next day to fly home, but he quickly nixed that. He said I was not to fly or drive for two weeks. He then added, "I've given you a shot of Heparin, a blood thinner. You're going to be here for a while. If all goes well, you'll learn how to give yourself shots of Coumadin, possibly every day for the rest of your life. It's the only way to keep your blood from clotting again."

I was too tired to even think about it. At 3:30 AM, I told Jan I would be okay and that she didn't have to stay any longer. I thanked her for coming and the help she provided. I knew that she had to be exhausted.

The next morning, I had breakfast and felt much better. I was allowed to shower and shave, which went well. I felt great until I climbed back into bed and was hooked up again. All of a sudden, my side started hurting just as a pulmonary specialist walked into the room. He told me to get used to it, this could continue for quite a while. Again, I was told that I was not out of the woods yet. Thankfully, the doctor was wrong, it never happened again.

My fear that night was hurting others through a tragic accident, which didn't happen. As the Apostle Paul said, *"For to live for me is Christ, and to die is gain."* (Phil 1:21 ESV) In a way, not being promoted to be with the Lord was disappointing, but that thought didn't last long.

I had dodged a bullet, but also knew that whatever was wrong with me was very serious. I began to wonder if I would really have to give myself shots every day. Fortunately, that would not be the case. It would have been difficult, considering my work schedule and travel. However, a new drug in pill form was working well with people that travel a lot. It also worked for me.

During the five-day hospital stay, Jan visited me every day. It was good to have a sister and her family in the area. That in itself was a miracle! She arrived the next morning at the same time three pulmonologists entered my room. They came to inquire about my work life. I told them of my busy travel schedule, which would possibly increase. They said, "Travel, especially flying and/or driving is out temporarily." They also added that when flying more than two hours, I must get up and walk to keep from clotting. They said to stop every two hours when driving long distances and walk for about twenty minutes.

The two-week prohibition from driving or flying meant I had to remain in Pennsylvania. Going back to Pittsburgh because of my ticket was no longer an issue, my recovery was.

I called Sherri to tell her what the doctors had said. I think at that point, the seriousness of my condition finally hit her. She was able to book a flight to Dulles Airport for the next day. I was walking the halls when she arrived. I heard her call my name behind me. At that moment, seeing Sherri again was wonderful!

Meanwhile, the doctors had decided to put me on a fairly new drug. It is a more stable blood thinner than Coumadin and is in a one-a-day pill form. That sounded good to me, and it was good for me. I began taking it the next day. Within seven months, I was taken off it completely. Continuing to walk twice a day really helped my recovery.

Once Sherri arrived, I felt a lot better. When I was released, she drove us back to Cranberry Township. We stayed with a wonderful couple from our Wexford church until I could fly again. While there, I called my doctor. He knew about my hospitalization and wanted to see me. I told him that he could not have known that I had a blood clot. It was apparently in my left foot, which could formerly not be scanned with ultrasound. Back then, a good picture of the veins in the foot was not possible. Today, however, feet can be scanned. I had it done recently.

It was my intention to assure him that he had checked everything and there was nothing to suggest otherwise. There was no neglect at all on his part, which I wanted him to know. To me, he is also a good friend. To him, I was something more than that.

When I told him about having coughed up blood, he said, "That was the beginning of the infarction." I asked what happens to the clots once in the lung. He said, "They are either ingested or coughed out, but they do not return to the circulatory system."

I said, "That's good news. This was a God story. It could have happened in any one of twelve cities, but it didn't. It occurred near Carlisle, where Jan lives. I can't thank her enough for helping in discovering the problem. God used her to save my life."

He added, "It definitely is a God story, John, you shouldn't be alive. When something like this happens, most people die because of larger clots or the length of infarction time. You should have died from heart strain long before it was determined what you had." That also confirmed what my pulmonary doctors had said in Carlisle.

At that point, I discovered the other reason he wanted to see me. He asked, "John, do you have time to talk with me a while longer? You are my last patient today, so I have a free hour." I was a bit surprised by that but was curious enough to ask what he had in mind.

He said, "I want to talk with you about God. I have only three people in my practice that I know I can talk to about Him, and you are one of them." I was eager to hear what he had to say.

He asked, "Can you explain to me what is meant by 'Christ's finished work on the cross'?" I said, "I'd be glad to. You may remember from the gospels that one of the seven phrases Jesus said on the cross was, 'It is finished.'" He said that he did know that.

I explained that Jesus was referring to having paid it all at the cross for the sins of the world. He had told the apostles that once He was lifted up, He would draw all men unto himself. That meant that the penalty of our sins had been completely erased by the cross. Those who would receive Him as their personal Savior and Lord would be saved by grace through faith alone.

He then told me that he was a member of a strict religious denomination. He had thought that they believed Christ paid it all for our salvation, but there was a difference. It seemed to him that the church, over time, had added many works as a qualification for salvation.

I asked him if he would like to pray, and we did. He's a believer, there's no question of that. I think he came to faith before he talked to me, but if so, God used me to help confirm it.

Unfortunately, I didn't live in the area any longer. Otherwise, I would have taken him to a great Bible study led by Dr. Bruce Bickel, an incredible Bible teacher and long-time friend. Men from one hundred churches located in four states drive to Christ's Church at Grove Farm every Friday morning to hear about a relationship with Jesus, not religion.

When I left my doctor's office, I stood by my car and looked upward. I said to Jesus, "Did all of this happen to confirm my doctor's salvation? If that's the case, it was worth it."

I thank the Lord for working in and through me during that divine appointment, regardless of my personal consequences. Whether my doctor was right or wrong concerning his church's doctrine, what the Bible says about Christ's finished work on the cross is true. We aren't saved by anything but grace through faith in Christ alone. That's the simplicity of the gospel. It's simple enough that even a child can understand it.

Nothing can be added to what Jesus did at the cross, and nothing can be taken away from it. He's not a discount ticket or Santa Claus who depends on our good deeds to acquire His gift. A gift is not something we earn; it's freely given. Salvation by faith is also a gift to be given freely to others. God generally uses us through our testimony to add new believers to the church.

Jesus is the eternal God who freely gives us the faith to receive the wonderful grace that He earned on our behalf at the cross. Unfortunately, most people reject Him, which literally breaks my heart, I know it breaks His. The Lord died to give us such a great salvation through a direct relationship with Him by faith. It's free to anyone who wants it.

Jesus has been building those relationships, one person at a time for almost two thousand years. The believers, over the centuries, are now a rather large number, and it's still growing. My hope is that those who may not yet know Christ will receive Him. He tells us, *"Take My yoke upon you and learn from Me, for I am gentle and lowly in heart, and you will find rest for your souls. For My yoke is easy and My burden is light."* (Matthew 11:29–30 NKJV)

That's a great offer!

The entire event was a miracle. After twelve trips, it happened in Carlisle where my sister lives and not somewhere else. Through her question to the doctor, I wasn't released with the incorrect diagnosis. That saved my life. Overall, I received great treatment, the information as to what happened, the prescribed medication, and how to avoid another episode.

Thankfully, my question to the Lord had been answered—no, it wasn't time to go home.

"For to me to live is Christ, and to die is gain"
(Philippians 1:21 NKJV)

The Canyon School Saga

CHAPTER 24

The Presidential Honor Guard

The next group of miracles occurred at a Canyon school in Southern California. It was a K-8 school with a very modest enrollment. Gary and I taught in portables, while the lower combination grades were taught in the only permanent facility. My class was a combination of grades four to six while Gary's was grades seven to eight.

The first of these miracles occurred during my second year there. It was the formation of a sixteen-girl "1776 Drill Team." The formation took two years to accomplish, but that wasn't the miracle. The miracle was the way it came together and the many events that followed. But first, I have to lay the background for all of what happened prior to that time.

During the late '60s, I served my country as a member of the Army. If my military training had come from my original orders to work in a psychology clinic at Fort Lee, VA, none of what follows could have happened. However, those orders had been cancelled because I had signed up for Officer's Candidate School (OCS). That was done, unwittingly, as a precaution in case I received unwanted orders after basic training. If that happened, I thought I could deny them in favor of the orders I originally received. I then found out how the military really works.

There was no such thing as a precaution like that. Four of us made that mistake at the Fort Jackson reception station before going onto basic training at Fort Gordon, GA. Instead of working and getting good experience in our college majors, we ended up in the infantry to prepare for OCS. Looking back on it now, though, I am very happy with what happened.

In addition to my infantry training, I became a member of our battalion basketball team at Fort Ord, CA. That determined where I would serve after Advanced Infantry Training (AIT). My company commander asked me to play on that team with him. It was through him that I received very good orders. I was given the privilege of serving in the Presidential Honor Guard, in which the same company commander had served before he attended West Point.

The Honor Guard Company was one of five companies of the Old Guard, Fort Myer, Virginia. The Old Guard, the oldest infantry unit in the country, was started by George Washington.

I became a member of the US Army Drill Team (also known as the Old Guard Army Drill Team). The Honor Guard Company was Company E at that time. Our platoon, the first platoon, was the marching platoon, drill team, and color team. We marched in parades, funerals, White House ceremonies, tomb ceremonies, and any other ceremony asked of us. But, the best part for me was the drill team, which has entertained people all over the country, perhaps the world.

We were basically professional marchers with the exception of two events: (1) the all-night mission of holding back the antiwar protesters during the march on the Pentagon, and (2) the riotous week in DC following the assassination of Dr. Martin Luther King.

The Martin Luther King assassination took us away from our mission. We set up cordons, or human barriers, to protect firemen as they fought flames of the burning buildings in the nation's capital. There were nine hundred fires set in Washington, DC, that week. Our squad went from one fire to another. There was a picture of me leading a squad down a DC avenue on the front page of a New York newspaper. It was not an experience to be recommended to anyone. As we reached a burning facility, we set up to face the onlookers. The intense heat of the flames was hard to bear. It felt as if our backs were about to explode. That is as close to hell as I will ever get.

The march on the Pentagon was shameful. It did not make sense, as we learned from the crowd. The male college students in the back of the crowd had pushed all of the young coeds up against us. We stood shoulder to shoulder while our officers and U.S. Marshals stood behind us. They kept track of where the concentration of bodies could possibly threaten our line.

One of the males in the back took a microphone to encourage the group to stay there and continue the protest. However, he said he couldn't stay to help them because he had a test the next day. Really! That told me a lot about the boys in the back and their commitment to a cause.

However, the young coeds were pressed up almost against us. One of them, right in front of me, asked if I would arrest her. She said, "I don't know if I agree with this anymore, but I really have to go to the bathroom. My problem is, I can't get out of here." Our problem was, we were ordered not talk with any of the protesters. Direct orders are not to be disobeyed.

When she saw that I was not responding, she began to accuse me of stoicism without any compassion or emotion. She was wrong, but I couldn't tell her that.

Suddenly she began to beat on my chest, but that didn't last long. A pair of large mighty hands reached over my shoulders to grab her by the coat and hair and yank her up over my head. When the thud of her body hitting the concrete was heard, I almost turned around.

Later, my company commander whispered in my ear that he was glad that I stayed in place. He was right. I understood why that was important. To have done otherwise would have made me part of the protest. That may have encouraged the crowd to break through the line and charge the Pentagon. Those who may have broken through and entered the Pentagon would have made the worst decision of their young lives. It's a good thing they never got past our line.

Outside of those two unforgettable incidents, the duty was somewhat hard but rewarding. Whenever a new person was assigned to our platoon, he (it was only men then) practiced to eventually become either a color team member or a drill team member. But first, everyone, after just two weeks in the platoon, became a part of the twenty-seven-man marching platoon for funerals.

In that short time, we learned to march without bouncing, keep our ranks straight and our arms swinging in unison. The rifle manual had to be smooth, with no jerking of the rifle or our bodies. We took all of this quite seriously by practicing every day in front of a mirror. We also used that body mirror to check out our appearance. We had to stand inspection before each job.

That meant shoes spit-shined so well our platoon sergeant could see his face in any part of them. Our shirts and uniforms, both blues and greens, had to be spotless and wrinkle-free; as did our fatigues for regular duty. In short, we seemed to be always ironing and shining.

When chosen for my first funeral, I was so nervous running to take my place in the platoon that I accidentally dropped my rifle. It somehow slid under a drain grating in the quadrangle. That is probably still the record for the dumbest maneuver in the history of the first platoon. Since that caused me to be late for formation, I flunked inspection. It's hard to pass inspection without a rifle. Of course, I was taken off that job right away and told to retrieve my rifle to practice for another job in the afternoon. I was ready for the afternoon job and even passed inspection. I never dropped my rifle or flunked an inspection after that.

It was an honor to be in the first platoon. I participated in some color team ceremonies early on, but later switched over to the drill team, which took a while for most of us to make. Once we did, it was exhilarating.

In my second year, I also became the right guide of the marching platoon. That meant that I had the pleasure of leading the platoons of all branches of the services onto the White House lawn, where the president would greet foreign heads of state.

I would also lead the platoons off and back to the Ellipse to dismiss them. Lyndon B. Johnson was the president then. When the president reviewed the troops, I was the first person he and the dignitary passed. As a young man then, it was hard to describe that feeling.

Once I had a few drill team performances under my belt, our platoon sergeant asked that I practice to be one of two throwers. Our job was to toss our rifles back over our heads from our two corner spots of the leading rank to the catchers at the rear corners' spots.

Two soldiers known as supernumeraries, or "supers," stood facing each other on each side of the platoon. As we marched between them, the catchers on each side of the rear rank tossed their rifles to them. Upon the command, "To the rear march!" we did the 180-degree turn to start back the way we came, but in slow cadence. While marching forward, we flipped our rifles over our heads to the catchers at the rear of the platoon.

The supers then flipped the other two rifles to us, which we caught with the hand of our inside arm. They had to flip the rifles just right for us to catch them correctly. As soon as we caught our rifles, the platoon returned to the cadence of 120 steps per minute as we marched off to end the performance.

Our platoon sergeant was as a very tough but fair leader. He never liked his first name or middle initial, so he just went by the name Big Jack. He expected us to perform flawlessly, no matter what the job or ceremony. He even said once, "I don't expect anything from you men but perfection." As a new member, I remember thinking, "Oh, is that all?" As time went on, I understood what he meant. One mistake could ruin the entire drill performance.

He pushed us to make the drill team. He knew the men he wanted, whether we liked it or not. His rule was this: Those who wouldn't cooperate or just didn't have it would be sent either to the Tomb of the Unknown Soldier or designated for assignment. The latter could have meant Viet Nam, although that would not have been his decision.

My final act in the Honor Guard before returning to finish college was Senator Robert Kennedy's funeral. During the week before the funeral, I was picked to be one of two honor-guard soldiers to be in the military deathwatch in New York before the body was to be transferred to Arlington Cemetery. However, at the last minute, the senator's wife decided to have a civilian deathwatch. Regardless, I considered it a great honor.

Our platoon was assigned to the gravesite in Arlington Cemetery. Anyone who worked the senator's funeral in any capacity received a personal thank you note from Ethel Kennedy. Mom was very proud of that.

In those days, I had an almost paralyzing fear of flying. When we are in a place where we have no idea what lies beyond our last breath, flying can be thought of as an unnecessary risk. At least it was for me. However, once I received the Lord, I began to love flying and do to this day. I even fall asleep sometimes. It's a great way to relax, get work done, do crosswords, read, or talk with those next to me. I usually end up doing the latter at some point in the flight. I've probably flown over a million miles since then. That, in itself, is a miracle. The verse, *"For God hath not given us a spirit of fear . . ."* (2 Timothy 1:7 KJV) I understand now but didn't then.

Unfortunately, back then, in other much riskier and more foolish areas, I did things without considering the consequences, which I definitely regret. Thanks to the Lord, He turned me around in many ways. He cleansed my heart and opened it to a totally different type of love. It was the love of Christ and the love of others. That is not always easy, but it's His way.

I also now know where my spirit will go when my physical body dies. It's completely up to the Lord to decide when and how. Therefore, I leave that to Him and don't worry about it or how it will happen anymore.

The Apostle Paul told us, *"We are confident, yes, well pleased rather—to be absent from the body and to be present with the Lord."* (2 Corinthians 5:8 NKJV)

That's quite an encouraging statement. It means, whenever the believer passes, it's a light-speed trip straight to Jesus. It is the twinkling of the eye, as Paul stated. I doubt that even our last breath gets completely out of our lungs before we are in His wonderful presence.

Once saved, I knew that He had work for me to do. And if that included flying, it was fine with me. It was a total change of mind and heart, considering how I felt while in my Honor Guard days. Only the Lord could do that.

The Lord would help me face the future and one of my favorite challenges of my teaching career. I never expected to use my military training again, but it became a huge part of Gary's challenge. I thank the Lord and Big Jack for—my Honor Guard experience.

"We walk by faith, not by sight." (2 Corinthians 5:7 NKJV)

CHAPTER 25

Gary's Request

The canyon was an interesting place in many ways, at least I found it to be. The people were friendly and their children were fun loving. It was, as one observer said, "The best of both worlds." For me, it was a great place to work.

My first year at the canyon school was a real learning experience. It was the fall of 1974, almost a year prior to God's hole-in-one. After Gary had come to know me a little, he asked me to share my Honor Guard service. I gladly shared my experience with my friend that day, and he seemed impressed. When he suggested that we form a school drill team, I was surprised but very pleased. That was a challenge I could handle, or so I thought.

With it being such a small school, it was difficult to envision the kids having any interest in my military marching experience. These were kids that often rode horses to school. The image of them performing a military-type drill was hard to picture. To make things worse, it wasn't that long after Viet Nam. Some canyon parents were not supportive of the war or the military.

I knew Gary's request would be a challenge. Therefore, in view of his enthusiasm for the project, I went for it. The best way to garner their interest was to demonstrate how an Honor Guard soldier marches without bouncing. Marching from one end of the portable to the other might do it, or so I thought. It didn't. Suffice it to say it was a very embarrassing moment!

The kids not only didn't like it, they booed. "None of you want to learn how to march?" I asked. That got me an emphatic and resounding "No!" What I had been proud of meant nothing to them. Being that there was no interest, I reported the result to Gary, and we forgot about it.

I did put together a boys' basketball team, made up of fourth to eighth-grade boys. Although I was somewhat less than a mediocre player in college, my military basketball experience helped me later. I played on two championship US Army Honor Guard basketball teams. Most of the players in the Old Guard league had also played in college, which made for great competition. And the gym was much longer and wider. I wasn't the best but had a lot of playing time. That was good experience for coaching in two different schools.

Our school team did fairly well, considering. When we lost, it was to bigger schools. However, their coaches were shocked to see that our team played in a well-disciplined manner, especially with fourth to sixth-grade kids playing alongside a few junior-high students. We didn't have many kids to choose from, but I felt good about what they learned that year. We wanted to do it again the next year. Sadly, we didn't have enough boys to put a team together that could compete.

With my newfound faith, I believed something was going to happen the next school year, and it did. Gary's request would get a different response. However, I never thought it would expand into a series of miracles to glorify God.

As the Bible says—**God may seem to be slow, but He's never late.**

"The Lord is not slack concerning His promise, as some count slackness"
(2 Peter 3:9 NKJV)

CHAPTER 26

The 1776 Drill Team

The next fall, soon after God's hole-in-one, Gary asked me to try the drill team idea again. My class had grown from sixteen students to twenty-three, and by this time, they knew me very well. Since two-thirds of my class consisted of the same students from the previous year, I agreed.

It occurred to me that, unlike the past year, better planning was in order. It had to be based upon something I didn't consider necessary the prior year—prayer. From beginning to end, the Lord had to be involved. Therefore, I asked the Lord to take over.

Presenting it to my class differently that year was easy. In explaining our goal, I said, "I want to develop a marching drill team with flags instead of rifles. It will be the best team in the entire school district." That was saying a lot. Our school district was very large and growing. In fact, we had the sixth best teachers' contract west of the Mississippi. It was a lofty goal, but with the Lord's help, we could do it.

With that in mind, I then said to the class, "Last year, you may remember that you were shown how to march without bouncing. Would you like to see that again?" They nodded, showing some interest this time, which was an encouraging sign. Our classroom that year was set up with two rows of desks facing two other rows along the length of the room. That left a big space in the middle for me to walk back and forth in between the rows. It worked out well, not only from a teaching standpoint, but also for what I did that day.

Once again, I marched from one end of the portable classroom to the other, between the opposing rows. Before I could ask, "What do you think?" they all applauded! It startled me, but it pleased me very much. Somewhat excitedly, I asked, "Would you like to learn how to drill?" This time, they all replied with a resounding "Yes!" From that, I knew the Lord was answering my prayer and that His hand was definitely upon us.

Learning to march is not easy for everyone. The first week, all but four boys and some of the girls dropped out. I established a color team with the remaining boys. But then the junior-high girls asked if they could join the younger girls. I was very pleased with that; they were the ones who had booed the loudest the prior fall. Adding them to the good marchers in my classroom gave the team exactly what we needed.

We practiced a short routine every afternoon in preparation for a proposed Christmas performance. I even had one of the girls design the drill to fit the limits of the performance area. We called it "Angie's Drill," which actually took place inside the canyon's fire department facility. Twelve of the girls picked it up fairly quickly. Four others showed promise but were not chosen for the first performance. That turned out to be a good thing. A sixteen-girl drill team would not have been able to fit. We had to use every inch of space we were given.

The team performed flawlessly to a stunned audience. They never dreamed the team could be that good. I know that Gary was also shocked at how good they were. I too was impressed, but I also knew what "Big Jack" would have expected, and we weren't there yet.

Still, I was very pleased with their performance and let the team know it. But a miracle would be needed if what I envisioned could work. If we wanted to win the annual Mission Viejo Spring Parade, things would have to happen which would be out of my control. That was the beginning of a series of miracles, which actually started the night at the firehouse.

The next spring would be 1976. Therefore, my prayer was for new colonial uniforms for the country's two hundredth anniversary.

That prayer was answered the next night, right after the firehouse performance.

A parent of one of my student marchers introduced herself by saying, "I'm Paula's mother. I sponsor a high school girl's drill team in Orange. Where did you learn to drill?"

I explained that I had marched with the best of the best in the military. I said, "The girls worked hard to learn the routine and performed very well tonight. However, we still have a lot of work to do." She replied that she couldn't believe how well disciplined they were. I was happy she had noticed.

What she said next grabbed my attention real fast. "You need uniforms, don't you?" I replied "Yes, I've been praying for that." She then said, "What kind of uniforms were you thinking of?" I said, "I would really like to have colonial uniforms for our country's two hundredth anniversary." She smiled and said, "Our high school ordered colonial uniforms for our girls, but they were too small. The company apologized and sent us the right order, while allowing us to keep the smaller ones. Would you be interested in them?"

I couldn't believe what I just heard! I said, "Of course, I'm interested, but how much will they cost"? Her answer took me by surprise. She said, "Paula told me what you were trying to do. I remembered the smaller uniforms and wondered if they would fit your girls. I asked my principal if I could give them to you. He said yes." And I thought—YES! God had answered in an incredible way. Each marcher of the now sixteen-girl drill team had a colonial uniform that fit her perfectly. You can't make this stuff up!

Gary saw that the drill team was doing really well, so he entered our team in the Mission Viejo Annual Parade. There were 115 entries, including a military drill team. In order to compete, I knew we had to have shoes with taps and metal strips known as cheaters. We needed shoes with heels thick enough to attach the cheaters to the inside of each heel. When the heels are clicked together, they make a great sound, especially when all sixteen clicks are heard at the same time. That makes a powerful impression.

After praying for the shoes, another mother came to me the next day. She told me that she saw a store in Orange that had girls' tap shoes on sale. That afternoon, we bused the girls to the store to try on the shoes. It was amazing. They actually had the right shoes with heels thick enough for the cheaters. And, they had the right sizes for everyone. Afterward, we found a cobbler who attached the cheaters. We were now ready to compete. The Lord had seen to that.

The shoes were perfect for doing the routine, but unfortunately, not necessarily perfect for marching a mile or more afterward. They had not been broken in yet, and some of the girls developed blisters while continuing to march along the rest of the parade route.

I doubt if it mattered to any of them, though. Even if they had known that blisters were a possibility, the team would have worn them anyway. They were very proud of what they had accomplished, and needless to say, so was I. I knew how far they had come.

Again, the girls performed flawlessly but with more confidence—so well, in fact, that that I could not envision losing the parade. You can imagine how that felt. However, once the parade had finished, no one reported anything to me. At first, I thought we had been overlooked or were not put into any competitive category. The only thing we heard after the parade was the obligatory "great job." I didn't know the actual results until ten o'clock that evening.

I was feeling somewhat disappointed until Gary's son called to say, "The drill team won the parade." We had even placed ahead of the military drill team.

For me, that would have been hard to believe if I hadn't known the Lord was in it. It was one the greatest feelings I could remember at the time. After all of the work we put in to take the prize, it was wonderful. It also meant that God had a far greater purpose than just winning a parade. By Monday, everyone was very happy when Gary related the results.

Gary signed us up for the school district's annual spring performance. Every school performed by grade levels in that show, we were an exception. At the end of our routine, the entire Anaheim Convention Center audience, over ten thousand cheering people, rose to their feet to applaud the 1776 Colonial Drill Team from our little canyon school.

Most people remember the movie about the little Indiana high school that won the Indiana State Basketball Championship. Looking back on all of it now, it was like Hoosiers for us but in a different venue. But, again, there was more.

The canyon held its own parade that summer. At the parade's end, all of the entries were judged for first, second, and third place. We again won first place among all the contestants. The real miracle was not winning the parade, we expected to win it. It was much more than that.

Many of the canyon people had heard that I was a born-again Christian. Some came to me and asked me about my faith. I gladly answered them, but then realized that the Lord was giving me an even better idea.

After getting Gary's consent, I asked Pastor Ron if we could invite the drill team and their parents to a Sunday church service. Afterward, we would have a performance of the boys' color team and then the drill team. That would be followed by a picnic and fun for all. We did that, and it was incredible. I'm not sure we could have done the same thing today.

God had finally answered Gary's challenge concerning the 1776 Sixteen-Girl Drill Team, and it was worth the wait. However, there was still a surprise awaiting me.

"And God is able to make all grace abound toward you, that you, always having all sufficiency in all things, may have abundance for every good work." (2 Corinthians 9:8 NKJV)

CHAPTER 27

The Divine Accident

During the church picnic, one of the fathers, who had recently separated from his wife, offered his congratulations to me for the team's success. I told him that it was all the Lord's doing. He said, "I don't agree with your premise, but it's amazing to see how good they are."

In those days, when someone challenged me in that spirit, I would immediately give them my testimony, including God's hole-in-one story. This case was no exception. Like most listeners, he couldn't refute any of it, but politely walked away with his head down. I never really expected to have a substantive conversation with him after that, but it happened.

After an outdoor school program one spring evening, he came to me again. This time, it was to ask me if I would visit his estranged wife. When I asked why, he replied, "I need you to tell her your story. She needs help." That really stunned me! He was an atheist but still wanted me to tell her about God because she needed help? In other words, he was saying, "Go ahead and lie to her, but for all the right reasons." He probably didn't see it that way, but regardless of his motive, I agreed to help. I was struck by the fact that he still cared for her. Maybe there was hope.

The reason for their separation doesn't matter, but something had happened the night before that could only have been the work of the Lord. It had noticeably shaken him in such a way that it was too much for coincidence. In fact, that was exactly what he said when he requested that I meet with her. It was why he came to me for help.

He had been at a bar in his area while, at the same time, his estranged wife had also been drinking, but at bar in a different community. While driving to their respective homes early the next morning, they actually collided with each other at an intersection. Neither was hurt, but it made him think. What are the odds that two separated spouses would smash into one another on the way to their homes in different communities? I don't know which one ran the light, but it's a moot point, one of them did.

I met with some of my Christian parents to ask them to pray for me during my meeting with his wife, which they did gladly. Their prayers were powerful. It was like someone had put a hedge around me when I walked into her home, and especially when we talked.

After she welcomed me, I saw that she wasn't alone. An older gentleman neighbor was there. As we talked for a little while, the subject of the Bible came up. He told me he knew the number of elders seated in heaven. At the time, that number, twenty-four, was news to me, but it helped set the stage for what I needed to tell her. Once he left, she said that she was really impressed with how much he knew about the Bible.

I explained that I was concerned for her two daughters, whom I loved in the Lord, as I did all of my students. She needed to know that the younger one was not doing well. She was having trouble with the separation and was concerned for both parents, especially after the unusual accident. If it had been worse, the girls and their brother could have been parentless.

I let her know that I once had a problem with drinking, but that God had done something miraculous about it to get my attention. I said that there was no doubt in my mind that the accident had been given to her for the same reason. After she thought for a moment, she agreed.

She really couldn't get over the accident. That, with what her friend had said about the Bible, had startled her. The two seemed to dovetail with why I was there.

I then gave her my testimony, followed by an invitation to receive the Lord. I asked her if she would like to know the God who loves her more than any person ever would. She said, "Yes."

She then prayed with me to receive Jesus as her personal Savior and Lord. The next morning, I told both of the girls what God had done with her. Both girls smiled happily, and that was enough for me.

I don't know if the parents ever got back together. Divorce is a terrible thing, and I hoped it could be avoided. Whether it was or not, I know that it was the Lord's clear message to them through— the divine accident.

But, as you may have guessed, there was still more to come.

"And I, if I am lifted up from the earth, will draw
all peoples to Myself." (John 12:32 NKJV)

CHAPTER 28

"In Jesus's Name," Miracles

There was a woman in the canyon who was a "Good News Club" teacher. Like other Good News Club teachers, she would meet with elementary children in her home after school to teach them about Jesus. She'd heard about my conversion and invited me to share my testimony with the children. I gladly agreed.

Once in the door, it surprised me to see my entire class sitting there, along with many others. After giving my testimony, I wondered if that was the right thing to do, considering their ages. Then again, they were used to problems occurring because of alcohol and drugs in the canyons. But, I still wasn't sure how they would handle it.

The Lord obliterated that concern the next morning. Each one of my students walked by my desk to tell me they had prayed to receive the Lord after I left. Because of what I'm about to relate, it was a good thing. It was a tremendous blessing not only to the club's teacher but also to me. Both of us knew how much God loved them. That love was definitely confirmed to one of the younger students in an incredible way.

Not long after that day, there was a fire in the canyon, and it was approaching the school. We were concerned that the flames, moving from tree-to-tree, might jump the campus fence and set our portables on fire. One of my fourth-grade students decided to stay near me as the fire approached. She was the younger daughter of the woman with whom I had prayed at the request of her estranged husband. We were standing by the fence outside our portable classroom waiting to see what was going to happen. I told her to pray, which she did. I did too!

We were watching the oak trees burning on the lot outside of the fence. Most were not close enough to threaten the school facilities. However, there was one tree that could spread its flames to a tree just outside the fence. Of course, our prayer was directed at that particular tree. We asked the Lord to protect it from the flames close to it.

Suddenly that tree exploded in flames. Without thinking, I screamed, "Go out, in the name of Jesus!" And it did, but for only a few seconds. Then, when the flames appeared a second time, I repeated the command, but this time added, "In the name of the Lord Jesus Christ." The tree immediately went out again, and this time it stayed out. I don't even think the leaves were scorched, but I can't say that for certain. I do know that the fire didn't kill the tree.

I looked at my young fourth-grade student to see if she was okay. Obviously, she was shaken. Her eyes were as wide as saucers. I said, "God heard our prayer." She, still stunned by what happened, nodded slowly in agreement. I'm sure she has never forgotten it. Obviously, I haven't!

A similar incident occurred not long after that, and it was just as uncomfortable. The mother of one of my students wanted to witness the love of Christ to a woman who owned a kennel of Saint Bernard dogs. I will never forget this one, and no one else would have either.

The student's parent asked me to accompany her in sharing the "Good News" of the gospel. We walked up a very long curved driveway to her friend's home and knocked on the door. When there was no answer, we turned to leave. At that moment, Saint Bernard Dogs, housed in a huge pen located in the back and just beyond the far end of the house, started barking. Ordinarily, that would have been no cause for concern. A very high fence kept the dogs separated from us.

However, one Saint Bernard became much more riled than the rest, so upset that it did something I still cannot believe. The angry dog somehow jumped up and pulled itself over the high fence, dropped to the ground, and ran full speed at us. I stepped in front of my student's mother and tried the same thing that had worked at the tree of fire.

Why? Was I feeling confident that I now had a formula for creating miracles? Of course not! There isn't any formula for creating miracles. But we sure needed one, and the Lord knew it. What man cannot do, God can, and He did.

I chose that option because I didn't know what else to do. So, I commanded that dog to stop, in the name of the Lord Jesus Christ. Once again, the Lord intervened. The dog stopped dead in its tracks, right in front of us. It even sat down, stopped barking, and stared at me.

Turning cautiously toward my friend, I said calmly, "Let's go," and we did. We walked slowly back down the long, curved driveway. The dog started to bark again when I looked back. We were relieved to see it still sitting in the same place. That was one of the longest walks of my life; at least it seemed that way. The dog's owner had to be perplexed when she returned home. Anyone would be startled to find that dog outside of the seemingly secure pen.

It had always been my understanding that Saint Bernard dogs were helpful, not a threat to humans. My research before writing this generally confirmed that. However, it also uncovered a story where one did become aggressive and started snapping at people. If the dog in question continued to finish what it started out to do, it would have been worse than just snapping. All we knew was that something got into this one. As angry as that dog was, it could have torn us up. Only the Lord could have prevented that from happening.

I wondered later, what could make an otherwise docile animal become that vicious? We know that Jesus, the apostles, and disciples cast out demons. Whatever it was, it's comforting to know that *"Greater is He that is in you than he that is in the world."* (1 John 4:4, Berean Study Bible)

I would submit from what I saw that day, God is definitely greater than anything that's in the world—even an angry, normally docile Saint Bernard dog!

What had happened from the entire drill-team saga, I believe, paved the way for God's real motive. The Christian parents met with me one day and made a special request. They asked if my pastor and I would start a Bible study with interested parents and other canyon residents. We agreed to do it.

The mother whom I'd accompanied to the kennel and her husband provided their house and food for the study. We met on a weekday evening, every week throughout the summer. That must have been God's intention in the first place. And he used all of the canyon miracles to create enough interest to make it happen.

The mother that had prayed to receive the Lord with me came to the weekly studies, along with the Christian families that made the request. To be able to talk about and praise God for the miracles we'd witnessed together and the Bible teaching that ensued was a blessing. During those two years, I learned the meaning of:

"Do not cease to cry out to the Lord." (1 Samuel 7:8 NKJV)

CHAPTER 29

Time to Go On to Next Town

Toward the end of that school year, I decided to read the Gospel of Mark for my daily Bible reading. At Mark 1:38 KJV, it seemed that the Lord was speaking directly to me. It read, *"And He said to them, 'Let us go on to the next towns,'"*

No! I am not comparing myself to Jesus; I am like Peter after the resurrection in that regard. It is believed that Peter dictated his gospel to Mark, which would make sense. Mark's gospel moves quickly from one event to another, and never focuses on Peter.

He never wanted to be on the same stage with Jesus. Even though we know he walked on water after the Lord beckoned him to come, that event is found in another gospel. If someone tried to worship Peter, he would pull him up and confess that he was just a man like him. That meant he was a sinner like the man trying to worship him. It also meant he wasn't Jesus. It is also believed that when he was executed, he asked to be crucified upside down so that no one would think he was Jesus. He doesn't even explain to Mark his part after the resurrection in the last chapter, as other gospels do.

I understand that. No one preaching the gospel should ever want people to believe they were anything other than imperfect. Peter was consistent in that. As an average Christian, I feel the same way. Christians are eternally forgiven but are not sinless. However, we try to sin less.

I would be lying, however, if I didn't say the phrase—let us go on to the next town—jumped out at me. Was the Lord sending me to another school? After mentioning this to my wife, she said, "I don't think that will happen. The Lord knows you love the canyon, your students, their parents, and your ministry with Pastor Ron. He won't send you somewhere else. Gary and you work well together. He would never want you to leave." But then she thought for a moment and said, "If the Lord wants you to leave, ask Him to tell you through Gary." That sounded like a plan, and I prayed with that purpose.

The Lord's answer didn't take long. On the way to school the next day, Gary said to me, "There is a new elementary school opening in the district next year." When I asked where it was located, he said, "It's only ten minutes from your house."

Because of my discussion with my wife, Gary got my attention. He continued, "You are welcome to teach with me as long as you want, but the new school would be very convenient for Donna to drop you off before going on to work." He was right! By that time, my wife worked at our kids' Christian school in Capistrano Valley, which would have been better for both of us.

When Gary continued, "The new school's principal is recruiting his staff, and he'd like you to interview for the fifth-grade gifted class position." My thought only took a moment. It was too much for coincidence. Gary knew how much my teaching in the canyon meant to me, and that leaving was never my desire. After conveying that to him, I said, "Considering what you said, I have to interview." Gary asked, "Why?"

I told him about my Bible reading and discussion with my wife. I added, "She said to have God speak through you." By this time, I don't think Gary was too surprised after seeing the miracles that had happened to me since my conversion. However, it must have had some effect.

After the interview, Gary said they were very impressed with me and the job was mine if I wanted it. I said, "I don't want to leave here, Gary, but now there's no choice; I have to accept." Teaching summer school would be my last experience with that incredible place.

A Christian mother of one of my best students called me, wanting to know why I was leaving. When I told her the story, she said, "I totally understand—***You have to go!***"

CHAPTER 30

Impressions

I've heard many Christians over the years say things like, "The Lord told me" or "The Holy Spirit said to me" before sharing something about their life or relationship with God. To some Christians, it may mean they heard an audible voice.

However, if God has ever talked to me audibly, I missed it. And, unless He insists, I prefer to leave it that way. Trusting in voices, in my opinion, is dangerous for two reasons. God speaks directly to us through His Word. It's His still small voice. The second reason is simple, what we think is God talking to us may be from the other side.

Some of those Christians I have encountered said they check what they have heard with Scripture. That's a great idea, but one must be certain that what they heard syncs with the context of a possibly supporting verse or verses. That could be difficult to do.

In biblical times, the Lord spoke audibly to His prophets. Of course, for every true prophet of God, around one hundred false prophets competed with him. As previously mentioned, they were generally astrologers, or seers. Bad things happened when kings consulted false prophets.

Born-again Christians trust God to speak to their hearts through His Word. I am one of them! When I read a verse, which seems aimed at me, it often comes from the pulpit the next Sunday. Sometimes it comes from the other teachers in our adult class. It may also come from our Bible study teacher. And, when it happens, the complete meaning of the verse confirms the Lord speaking to me.

The Mark 1 verse related earlier, for me to go on to the next town, was confirmed by my friend Gary. He was completely unaware of it, but the Lord was reaching me through not only His Word and my wife, but also through my friend.

However, on rare occasions, I have received impressions. It's like someone starting to say something we seem to know in advance. No matter how often, it is what I call an impression. Sometimes, those impressions became fulfilled through miracles, or at least, acts of providence. For example, I once sent an email to a friend who quickly replied, "I was writing the same thing to you."

When we had been on solid ground with God's Word after the first year of our Christian walk, something very unusual happened. After a pizza night at our favorite restaurant, we headed home. However, instead of going straight through the light to get to our house, I made a left turn.

My wife and kids asked what I was doing, but I didn't know. For some reason, it seemed like the right thing to do. I said that we'll turn right at the next light and take the long way home. However, when we got to the light, there was someone sitting on a bench waiting for a bus. The person had her head down and seemed to be crying.

I don't know who said it first, but one of us said, "Isn't that Chris's wife?" our friend from church. I pulled our van over and called to her to get in with us. She did, and we continued on to one of our favorite ice-cream parlors.

In the parking lot, she told us that she was asked to leave her home and family, and in not a kind way. She and her husband, formerly separated, had recently come back together. The reason for the argument that led to her being put out of the house is not important. I said, "Let's get some ice-cream and go back to your house. Our kids can play with yours, you can talk with Donna, and I'll talk with Chris." I can't remember what we said. It was probably what God thinks concerning marriage, I guess, but I'm not certain. It was enough for Chris to realize that this was a work of the Lord.

He and she happily got back together and told us that the next Sunday at church. One may think that it wasn't a miracle; people run into friends like that all the time.

Although she was a friend in trouble, I could agree with that. However, why did I turn left? I knew the way home was straight ahead. I was tired, but not enough to make that mistake.

In fact, I never made it again. Every time I would go through that intersection on the way home, I would think about our friends whose marriage was saved that evening. That had to be the Lord's doing.

> *"The Lord knows how to deliver the godly out of temptations."* (2 Peter 2:9 NKJV)

Part III

Miracles of Others

Chapter 31

Introduction to the Miracles of Others

I don't want anyone to get the impression that I'm the only one to have experienced miracles or acts of providence. Most born-again Christians have had something happen that they could not explain. However, most people don't want to believe miracles happen, even the clergy.

John 10, listed below, deals with Jesus exhorting the leaders that wanted to put Him to death. Jesus was known for many miracles, of which the Pharisees were well aware. Many of them had witnessed a few of them. However, they still asked Him to tell them plainly if He was the Messiah. Jesus responded, *"I told you, and you do not believe. The works that I do in my Father's name bear witness about me, but you do not believe because you are not among my sheep."* (John 10:25–26 ESV)

In verse 38, he finishes with, *"Even though you do not believe me, believe the works, that you may know and understand that my Father is in me and I am in the Father."*

This is another proof text that Jesus is God, the second person of the triune God. However, the Pharisees and scribes didn't want to accept the truth of anything He said or did. Jesus was a threat to their power and control over the people. Even though they hated the Romans, they had a good thing going. The Romans had allowed them to rule over their people as long as their rule didn't conflict with Roman law. Believing Jesus to be their Messiah could change that.

Once Jesus resurrected and ascended to the Father forty days later, He continued to work his miracles through the apostles and disciples. He also worked through converts such as priests, Pharisees, scribes, and ordinary Christians for the next two millennia.

He is still doing that today. However, just as Jewish leaders rejected Him and His miracles in their day, the world rejects Him the same way today. Many are skeptical of professed miracles, some of which may be refutable.

Religious charlatans and some giving false testimony about dying and going to heaven, only to be sent back, have muddied the waters in that respect. It may even be why some doubt the miracle of the Apostle Paul in Acts 14:19–20. After being stoned to death by professionals, his spirit went to heaven. However, God sent him back with the admonition that he was never to say what he saw there. He not only returned, but his bloodied and broken body was completely healed. He confessed it fifteen years later.

Whether or not that has happened to anyone since, it will always be obscured by the many false testimonies of a similar experience. Skepticism often wins out in those cases.

However, with those miracles people cannot refute, there should not be skepticism. Unfortunately, it is those which many do not want to hear. Though they are irrefutable, most people will never accept them as true. They do the same with the many fulfilled prophecies, which is a shame. In actuality, they are saying, "I don't want to believe in miracles or God."

This book does have some autobiographical material just by the nature of what the Lord has done through me. Although some sections may seem that way, this book is not about me. It's all about the awesome God we serve. When it comes to personal miracles, I'm more of an observer. The Lord's miracles and the reasons for them are the book's point. However, I am definitely not alone when it comes to experiencing His miracles. Upon his miraculous return to Congress recently, Representative Steve Scalise said, "Miracles do happen!" He is living proof!

I submit that miracles happen to many believers and even nonbelievers. One happened to me as a nonbeliever. Jesus told us that once He would be lifted up, He would draw all people to Him. It is, therefore, reasonable to assume that He draws us to Him in whatever way He wants. Usually, it's through believers, but not always. God did miracles through Judas when he went out with the twelve. However, he wasn't a believer in the way we are. He didn't trust, rely, and depend upon the Lord for everything. Judas had an agenda of liberation theology. He believed that God would send His Messiah to free the Jews from Roman oppression. He was wrong!

The Lord's reasons for drawing all people to Him through miracles are (1) they are designed to glorify the Father and His Son; (2) God draws people to receive Him as their Savior and Lord; and (3) to show the "Never-Jesus" people there is no excuse for not receiving Him. Even though He can see that they will never receive Him, He still presents His offer of salvation to them.

This explains why one demon-possessed brother wanted to follow Jesus while the other apparently didn't. Jesus had cast out one thousand demons from each one of them. Like all people, both were sinners in need of salvation. However, considering the life-changing freedom they received, both brothers should have wanted to follow Him, but only one did. Sadly, this seems to be still the case today. With some, even miracles in their life will not convince them that God exists.

Once we are drawn to Christ and learn of His offer of salvation, it seems irresistible to one group, but to the rejecters, it isn't. Even if just two people understand His offer of eternal life, one may receive Him, but the other may not. That's not in every case, but I have seen it.

The receivers will see it as an incredible work of mercy and grace; the others will see it as an act of weakness, not worthy of their consideration. One person's spirit is born from above or born-again through faith; the other's is lost through the pride which rejects that doctrine. The born-again spirit of a new believer belongs to God forever. The lost person's spirit is kept from eternal life with God forever. The strange thing about this example is—both could be lifetime churchgoers.

All born-again believers are members of Christ's body, His church. If the rejecters remain lost until death, they send themselves to the only other place eternal spirits can go, Hades. The former group will be immediately with the Lord forever after they pass.

The latter group, one thousand years after His second coming (the Lord's return to earth), will stand judgment based on the Mosaic Law. These will get a chance to prove why they don't deserve eternal punishment, but it will not stand. Our decision for Christ must be prior to physical death.

There are two important things to understand here. First, by this time, the lost know that their banishment from God was because they were unrepentant sinners who didn't want to be with Him forever. The offer to receive Him was the same as it was for those who accepted it. However, even though they refused his grace, they will know His judgments are just. Therefore, they will have no excuse.

Secondly, even with what they have endured to this time, they will still not want to live in a perfect place occupied by a perfect God who died to blot out all of their sin and its penalty. They will never wish to live with those who put their trust in Him prior to physical death. Therefore, they will be found guilty and left to go to the one and only place a dead spirit can reside after judgment. It's the place of eternal punishment, which, while alive on earth, they chose over heaven. In reality, they, not God, will have sent themselves to hell.

One of the reasons for writing a book of God's miracles in my life and others is simply this—I don't want anyone plodding through a life of unrepentant sin to die before making the decision for Christ.

The miracles prove that Jesus is alive, and through believers, we witness to others that He is the Christ, the Son of the living God.

One may also say, "God is going to save those whom He wants to save anyway, so why does He need you or anyone else to witness His love and grace?" For two reasons: (1) He told us to witness and not only that, he said that once we receive the Holy Spirit, we will have the power to witness; (2) God says His good works through believers have been prepared beforehand that we should walk in them. Therefore, we must assume that when the time comes to witness, we will know it and do it. He seems to take over from there. That has always been true in my case.

From a practical viewpoint, and with all of the evidence of His deity, it would seem to me that all people would want to become that which we were truly created to be. Think about that! Everyone could enjoy all of the blessings which come with God's promises. Those who have placed their faith in the God that paid it all for their sins will discover God's true reason for their creation. I am looking forward to that which his *miracles* have confirmed.

If you have a picture of heaven with everyone lying around on clouds doing nothing forever, you've got the wrong picture. The Bible says we will reign with Christ for one thousand years. That isn't lying around, that's action. It's a wonderfully active life that will never disappoint in any way.

In addition, we are told by the apostles that we will know all things. That means we will be smarter than any other human that ever lived, except Christ. We will have the energy to do whatever our job demands. People have said, when one is having fun with his job, he really doesn't have a job. When we are with God during His thousand-year reign, whatever our job is, it will always satisfy. It's having the joy from being in a position to see His miraculous works. Here on earth, as we wait for the rapture and His millennial reign to begin, His joy in us strengthens our faith.

I imagine many readers, Christian or not, will acknowledge that there was a time when something happened to them which couldn't be explained naturally.

It is for those that I dedicate the following—**miracles of others.**

"Believe the works that you may know and understand." (John 10:32)

CHAPTER 32

Bob's Miracle

Robert, a Christian friend of mine, witnessed a miracle of one of his friends. Since his name was also Robert, in order not to confuse anyone, we will refer to the second Robert as Bob. Bob had an inoperable cancerous brain tumor. However, it wasn't the normal isolated brain tumor, this one was unique. It was more like an octopus, a feature that made it inoperable. The tumor, imbedded in his brain, was also wrapped around the optic nerve in one of his eyes. Bob continued to lose sight in the eye but also began to lose control of muscular function.

Bob's mother had died from exactly the same condition, which may point to some type of a genetic problem. Whether or not this was the case, Bob received the same prognosis his mother was given. If nothing changed, Bob's chances of long-term survival with this condition were poor, at best.

Robert and Bob were members of the Gideon Bible Society. Robert said that Bob was so zealous for his faith in Jesus that he and another Christian brother started a prison ministry. Over time, the inmates began to really respect Bob, who was used to lead many of them to the Lord. After a Sunday service at the prison, all of the new brothers in the Lord laid hands on Bob and prayed for healing. This is how Bob told the story to Robert:

"As the men began to pray, I felt a sharp pain move from temple to temple. The following week, I was scheduled to have an MRI as a last check to find the best way to attempt to operate. Even though the doctors had low expectations of a successful operation, they still had to try. However, when the MRI was conducted, they could not find any evidence of the tumor that they had found in an earlier procedure. The tumor was completely gone!" Bob's sight in the affected eye began to return slowly, along with his muscular function.

Praise God for miracles! When Robert met with Bob, he was fully recovered and giving all the praise and glory to our Lord Jesus Christ.

Thinking back to my friend Ron's healing miracle, this thought occurred to me, "How soon would I hear of a similar one?" I heard of one quickly after that but many since. However, while Ron's miracle saved him from a life-changing condition; Bob's miracle actually saved his life. It was God's will for Bob to continue ministering to those once considered the—"least of these."

I am grateful to Robert for sharing Bob's miracle and allowing me to put it in the book. I'm sure the men who prayed for his friend felt a joy like no other, as I did with Ron. God's miracles often focus intentionally on one person who would bring joy to many. These miracles strengthen the body of Christ through a deeper understanding of who the Lord is. Miracles like this serve to confirm our hope in the risen Jesus. But remember, all miracles are secondary to His Word.

Recently, in my adult Sunday-school class, one of our attendees told us of her friend's healing miracle. However, her friend emphatically told our class member it wasn't a miracle and that she should stop calling it that. What was it then? The friend couldn't say, but in her mind, miracles don't happen, and therefore, it couldn't be a miracle. She even told her friend, who prayed for her intently, not to contact her any longer. How sad! This serves to illustrate that one person can receive a miracle and praise God, while another will not accept that it is a miracle from God. As long as she is alive, the Lord can change her heart. Therefore, we still pray for her. However, we feel sorry for her. She deprived herself of the Lord's joy. That's missing a lot—***there is nothing like it!***

> *"Ask and you will receive, that your joy may be full."*
> (John 16:24 NKJV)

CHAPTER 33

You Rang, Lord?

This next miracle I cannot verify, but I have no reason to doubt its validity. I don't know any of the names or places. However, it was told to me years ago by someone very close to me, one of the highest integrity. She was watching Christian TV when she heard it.

A pastor/TV evangelist was being interviewed about miracles that he had witnessed during his ministry. Apparently, he was asked to share the most memorable one. I can't write the exact quotes the pastor used, but the story went something like this:

As he was preaching a message on his live weekly TV show, a woman, about to commit suicide, decided to first turn on her television. Somehow, it was tuned to the channel on which he was speaking. As she was listening to him, she decided that he was the kind of person she would like to meet before ending her life. At the end of his message, the pastor invited viewers to call his office if they needed help. At that moment, a number appeared on the screen. Quickly, maybe too quickly, the distraught woman wrote what she thought was the pastor's office number.

Once the program concluded, he left the studio to drive home. For whatever reason, the woman waited to make the call. Meanwhile, the pastor decided not to go straight home but stop at a restaurant. Later, when he went back to his car to continue home, something unbelievable happened. As he was about to get in his car, the nearby pay phone began to ring. At first, He didn't want to answer it, but something made him think he should.

When he did, he got one of the biggest shocks of his life. The person on the other end asked, if he was the pastor she had seen on television earlier? When she mentioned his name, he said "Yes! I am, but how did you get this number?" She said she wrote it down at the end of his message and finally decided to call him.

After looking at the number on the payphone, He told the woman that he would be glad to talk with her but the number that she had written down was not his office number but a pay phone's. He then explained his story of deciding to stop at a restaurant instead of going straight home as he usually would, which was why he heard the ring. He continued on to tell her that, for some reason, he felt that he was supposed to answer it.

The woman was floored by his story. Obviously, he was definitely the one she was supposed to call. She proceeded to tell him the reason. After she told him why she wanted to speak with him, both of them were certain that the Lord had moved him to answer the payphone. He then led her in a prayer to receive Jesus Christ as her personal Savior and Lord. Her life and its meaning completely changed after that. I can imagine the God-given joy that was shared by her, a new believer, and her new pastor. It was truly a divine appointment.

Miracles always have a purpose. This one shows the purpose God has for everyone who would believe in him by faith alone. She now had a reason to live and believe in the hope that is in us. Christ would touch many with her story. It definitely impressed my friend.

I can relate to this, but my testimony's circumstances weren't as bleak as hers. Her story was a lifesaver. It's the Lord's primary ministry to—save those who are lost. She was lost, all right, but not forever. The Lord had seen to that, and *in His miraculous way.* The following verse is taken out of context. For some strange reason, it just seems to fit.

"God will make you worthy of his calling."
(2 Thessalonians 1:11 ESV)

CHAPTER 34

Bill's Two Miracles

Bill, my friend since first grade, offered these two miracles in his life:

I can think of two cases offhand in my life when I felt there was divine intervention. Neither was earth-shattering. I wouldn't have died if the events didn't happen, but I definitely felt something out of the ordinary had occurred.

1. God's provision

The first was when my wife, Linda, and I were younger. Early in my career, we had agreed to have a new house built. First, though, we had to sell the house in which we lived. We did that, but as the new house was under construction, the sale of our first house fell through. It caused some financial stress, to say the least, especially with three kids under five.

My job often involved travel, this time, it was to St. Louis. In my hotel room, I took out the Gideon Bible from the night stand. While leafing through it, five hundred dollars fell out of the Bible. I went to the front desk to report what I found. The management checked all the people who had stayed in that room over the past several months, but not one had reported it missing. The hotel manager told me to keep it. As the Word says, The Lord provides what we need (Phil 4:19). In this case, it was literally provided—through His Word.

2.   God Does Answer Prayer

A few years ago, while at our winter home in Steamboat Springs, Linda broke her leg. She had an operation, but would have to endure the requisite rods, screws, etc. The surgery on a Friday was followed by what appeared to be a good recovery, which allowed her to come home on Monday. Thursday night, in trying to sit down on the couch, she broke it again near the original break. Back to the hospital! Because of the pain, she couldn't do the required physical therapy. The PT people would just stick their heads in the door to see her in bed and leave.

On the next Monday morning, the hospital management came to tell us she must leave. They said she had to go to a rehab center in Denver, 170 miles away, a trip Linda could not possibly have made. With her inability to do the PT at the hospital, we were told that our insurance required it, even if she wasn't strong enough to do it. Needless to say, Linda was beside herself.

With the ongoing commotion, I decided to go to the cafeteria. A man of faith came over to me who, I thought, was someone that liked to visit hospitals. In noticing my despair, he asked, "Are you all right?" When I told him the story, he said, "Let's pray for her," which we did. I thanked him and went back to the room, but Linda was not there. She had gone for a walk with the PT people!

When they returned, Linda said, "I just suddenly felt like I could get out of bed and, with a walker, perform what they required of me to be released to home care." The doctor signed the papers and back to our winter home we went, where Linda recovered over the next three months.

Coincidence? I don't think so. I think the guy in the cafeteria was an angel.

You may be right, Bill. The Word does say, *"Do not neglect to show hospitality to strangers, for thereby some have entertained angels unawares."* (Hebrews 13:2 ESV)

That has probably happened to all of us at least once. God does answer prayer!

Then, again, it may have been a volunteer chaplain or an ordinary believer strong in the faith. Either way, Linda received a healing miracle while you were praying.

Another biblical similarity is found in John's Gospel:

> *"So Jesus came again to Cana of Galilee where He had made the water wine. And there was a certain nobleman whose son was sick at Capernaum. When he heard that Jesus had come out of Judea into Galilee, he went to Him and implored Him to come down and heal his son, for he was at the point of death. Then Jesus said to him, "Unless you people see signs and wonders, you will by no means believe."*
>
> *The nobleman said to Him, "Sir, come down before my child dies!" Jesus said to him, "Go your way; your son lives." So the man believed the word that Jesus spoke to him, and he went his way. And as he was now going down, his servants met him and told him, saying, "Your son lives!"*
>
> *Then he inquired of them the hour when he got better. And they said to him, "Yesterday at the seventh hour the fever left him." So the father knew that it was at the same hour in which Jesus said to him, "Your son lives." And he himself believed, and did his whole household."* (John 4:46-53 NKJV)

One other note concerns Bill's first miracle. Obviously, someone, for some reason, put the money in the Bible. We have no idea why it was put there or how long it was there. Many people buy Bibles, but few read them. More read them in hotels or there wouldn't be a Gideon Bible Society. In any event, the Lord saw to it that Bill and Linda got the blessing.

These are great examples of the miracles of others. As I mentioned earlier, at some time after *God's Hole-in-One* is published, I hope to follow up with a book by the same name. It will be completely devoted to those who have sent their stories to me. In fact, I will provide a Website for anyone who would like to share their God stories with me and others. Just make sure they can be verified. The most interesting ones will go into that work. If I receive a lot of miracle stories, I may start a newsletter also by that name. It may help my brothers and sisters in Christ to step forward and glorify God by sharing His miracle working in their lives. The world, as it exists today, needs to hear them.

> *"God also bearing witness both with signs and wonders,*
> *with various miracles, and gifts of the Holy Spirit,*
> *according to His own will."* (Hebrews 2:4 NKJV)

Part IV

John Corfield's
Personal Testimony
of Faith in Christ

March 1–May 15, 1975

CHAPTER 35

Faith Comes by Hearing

It's time for my testimony of how I came to know Jesus Christ as my personal Savior and Lord. It also fits into the category of "I will never forget it" accounts. My coming to Christ wasn't borderline miraculous, it was definitely a real miracle. It was given to me by the all forgiving, loving, and only true God. Like all sinners, I didn't deserve His grace or the faith to believe it.

Consistent with what I've already written, it is His story, not mine. The miracles glorify our Creator who is *the same yesterday, today and forever."* (Hebrews 13:8 NKJV)

Prior to my conversion, Gary and I had been drinking buddies on Fridays. He and, usually, his wife would meet with me at our favorite watering hole for a great steak dinner. After that, we would drink beer until 2:00 AM. My wife, who hadn't yet become seriously ill, would sometimes hire a babysitter and meet us there.

After golf on Saturdays, I would go home because Donna usually worked at night or on weekends. Once the kids were in bed, I would start drinking beer again.

March 1, 1975, was one of those Saturday evenings. When I was relaxed, I turned on the television to find a good late movie. The only one was the Truman Capote film *In Cold Blood*, a true but sad and very scary story. Science-fiction movies in those days didn't bother me at all. Monster movies and creatures from outer space were fun to watch, but this story was true.

I had seen it once before with some friends on base at Fort Myer, Virginia. This night, though, the idea of seeing it again was not a good one. The story really frightened me, but admitting that to friends wasn't my way. Watching it alone was a different thing entirely.

Finding another movie was impossible. There wasn't much of a choice back then. No one had cable or satellite TV options in the bedroom communities. Cable did exist for those in rural or mountain areas, but they received only a few more channels than those with antennas. Having nothing better to do, I watched it. Bad decision! There were two six-packs in the refrigerator, and while being scared to death, I drank eleven cans. I'd have drunk number twelve too if I hadn't passed out on the couch just as the movie was ending.

This may be hard to believe, but we had only one key to our condo in those days. For some reason, we never saw a need for a second one. On this particular night, Donna had forgotten to take the key with her, but I wasn't aware of it. When she came home, the door was locked. She had to knock on the door for me to answer, but I didn't hear her knocking.

She kept trying, but again, I didn't answer. It took her half an hour of pounding on the door and ringing the doorbell for me to finally wake up and unlock the door. I opened the door, but without saying anything, made my way upstairs and passed out on the bed. Needless to say, Donna was irate, but she soon realized my condition and left me alone.

The next morning, the kids awakened me to get my permission to go to church with the neighbor kids. The way I felt, I didn't see why not. It meant more time to sleep. Donna had awakened early and was still angry when she dressed and went back to work for the day shift.

When I finally got out of bed, something very unusual happened. The usual cigarette was not my first choice. I had been asleep a long time and was really hungry. Eating a good breakfast was the only thing on my mind.

However, when I opened the refrigerator to get to the eggs and bacon, I noticed the one remaining can of beer. Usually, I could handle one can before Monday, but not this day.

I felt ill just looking at it. Very few hangovers were that bad. It wasn't the amount consumed but the short period of time it took. Once I closed the refrigerator door and began making my food, that feeling left, and everything went fine for the rest of the day.

The kids returned from church needing lunch. After sitting down to eat, I noticed that they were looking at me strangely. They apparently liked church very much. I wasn't sure how I felt about that, but I listened to them relate what it was like. Neither of them brought up what really happened there nor, thankfully, what had happened the previous night. If they heard the pounding on the door and doorbell that night, I definitely didn't want to explain it.

Donna returned from work about 4:00 PM and was now more tired than upset with me. I immediately apologized for the night before and told her what had happened. She listened but didn't say anything. When she discovered that she was out of cigarettes, she coldly asked me if I had one. I shook my head no, but I told her she could find my pack on my nightstand. She looked at me quizzically but, again, said nothing, and went upstairs to retrieve the pack. Perhaps she thought I had slept all day. The fact that the pack was almost full probably confirmed her suspicions, at least temporarily.

She returned to say, "It looked like you didn't smoke much today." It was then that I realized I hadn't smoked at all. That sickening feeling briefly returned while I explained that I just didn't feel like smoking or drinking. She said, "It must have been a really bad night!" She was right about that.

During that evening, the kids were still looking at me strangely. They were only six and seven years old at the time. I asked them what was wrong, but Tracee replied, "Nothing." I didn't pursue that line of questioning even though my hangover was almost gone. Beginning to feel like a normal human being again was welcome at that point; discussions weren't.

It didn't even occur to me to grab my cigarettes when awakened the next morning. I just had breakfast and got ready for work. Once Gary arrived to drive us to school, I said goodbye to all and left. Gary didn't notice that day that I wasn't smoking, but sometime later in the week he did. He and others asked if I was trying to quit. My only answer was, "I don't know, I just don't feel like it lately."

That Friday after school, I didn't join Gary and his wife at the bar. Instead, I told my wife I didn't feel well and went to bed. It felt like the flu, which caused me to also miss a few days the following week. When making the doctor's appointment, I couldn't say what was wrong with me, I really wasn't sure. Whatever it was, I felt terrible.

While relating this story to my doctor, he said that it was probably withdrawal symptoms from no longer smoking or drinking. He may have been right if fever and flu symptoms are a part of that experience. However, when someone goes through withdrawal, doesn't he usually know what he is experiencing and why? Doesn't he have an incredible urge for that to which he was addicted? I guess that should have occurred to me, but it didn't, not in any way. I didn't have any idea what the problem or remedy was. That's what sparked the doctor's visit.

Feeling better, I returned to work with a new outlook. It felt good to be sober. It had been over two weeks since my last cigarette or can of beer. Within another two weeks, all six of my school colleagues had noticed and asked me if I had quit. I affirmed that I had. When they asked me how I did it, I replied, "I don't know," and at the time, it was the truth!

Cigarette smoke began to bother me after a while, and, if possible, I avoided it. I began driving our van to school whenever I could, unless Donna needed it. One Friday afternoon, Gary did drive me home. However, instead of saying goodbye, he said, "If you have any guts at all, you'll go inside and get your money and come with me to the bar. Everyone misses you!"

I looked over at my friend and said, "I don't know why, but I don't think I will ever drink or smoke again. But if I ever do, it will be with you."

It's hard to say how he felt about that, but when I walked into the condo, I stopped to ask myself why I had just turned down a Friday fun time with Gary. At that moment, I thought of a Bible verse which had become important to me in an odd way. It reads:

"I am the way, the truth and the life, no one comes to the Father but by me." (John 14:6 NKJV)

That stopped me right in my tracks. It was a verse shared originally by a guitar player friend of mine. It was a year or so prior to meeting Gary. We had just finished a jam session at our Huntington Beach condo. The drummer, a different Gary, lived in the condo behind ours. He had introduced me to his guitar friend, George. Both were born-again Christians. However, George was the one on fire for Christ. He had come to know the Lord through the "Jesus movement."

George asked if I believed in Jesus. My reply, which rarely got a rebuff, was, "No, it's my belief that every man should believe in God in his own way. Besides, Jesus never said He was God." When he replied with John 14:6, he did get my attention, but I shrugged it off.

In retrospect, how I felt privately was a different story. Because I didn't know much about the Bible, I was surprised. The verse haunted me from that time on. Jesus claimed to be God seven times in Scripture, but I was unaware of it.

Jesus was on my mind the day Gary challenged me to get my money and accompany him to the bar. I began to wonder, "Has Jesus done this to me"? At that exact moment, there was a knock on my door. When I opened it, the pastor of the nearby Grace Brethren Church was standing on the porch, politely smiling at me. Before I could ask him who he was and what he wanted, he quickly introduced himself. In a friendly voice, he said, "I am Ron, the pastor of the church your children attend on Sunday." He went on to say something no one had ever said to me: "I would like to talk with you about your personal relationship with Jesus Christ."

His question stunned me! Many had asked me if I believed in God, but no one had ever talked about a relationship with Jesus. Had I not been thinking about Jesus at that moment, I would have politely said that I wasn't interested and closed the door. But not that day!

By this time, my wife was standing at the top of the stairs looking down at me. She told me later that, knowing my view of religion, she was afraid I would throw him off the porch. What made her come to that conclusion is still a mystery. I would never do that to anyone for any reason. Instead, I said to him, "Something very strange has happened to me, and maybe you have the answer." With that, I motioned for him to enter.

When he saw my upright piano, he asked if I would play something for him. It's doubtful that I did, I usually don't play for anyone but family and friends. Anyway, my interest was more in relating my unusual experience. Therefore, I explained everything that had happened.

I really don't remember his exact response. It seemed to be some type of confirmation that the Lord was doing a work with me. In fact, after my conversion, he told me that when he got home that day, he said to his wife, "The Lord was already there when I arrived."

He didn't stay long, though. Since he had to get home, he left a Christian tract. However, it was about the Holy Spirit, not Jesus or the Four Spiritual Laws. Pastor Ron was out of those. The Holy Spirit was the one person of the triune God about *whom* I knew absolutely nothing.

That's not completely true. I did know that His symbol was the dove. It was during our confirmation evening in eighth grade. Our minister had told me to give that answer in response to his question, "What is the symbol of the Holy Spirit?" All of our parents were in attendance and seemed to enjoy that we all gave the right answers to his questions.

Before he left, Pastor Ron asked if he could visit me again. Even though I didn't know much more about Jesus than I had already known when he showed up, I welcomed the thought.

He had also invited me to come to church, but I politely said, "Maybe some time." I did agree that Troy and Tracee could keep attending. That would have never happened prior to my strange experience. When he left, I tried reading the tract but didn't understand it at all. Thankfully, that would soon change.

Instead of golf on Saturday, I had recently registered to monitor a jazz piano class. Sunday morning without the kids had become my time to practice. I'd also acquired an electric piano, which, with earphones, I could play as loud as I wanted without bothering the neighbors. That silenced my neighbors' complaints. My practice on my slightly out-of-tune upright was apparently driving them crazy.

I'm not certain how soon Pastor Ron visited me again, but he brought the right tract that time. Although he talked to me a little bit about Jesus, he seemed to be more interested in my background. I can't remember whether it had to do with church background or just background in general.

But we did go through some of the tract. When he left this time, I still didn't have all of the answers, but somehow felt that, through him or his ministry, my answers would come. The new tract began to make sense and was helpful, but I must have been interrupted while reading it. I hadn't read the last part where the sinner's prayer could be found.

One Sunday morning, the neighbor's daughter knocked on the door to invite me to church. She told me that I might like to hear the special guest speaker. I thanked her for thinking of me but declined in favor of piano practice.

I practiced all day, with meals being the only exception. When she returned in the afternoon to invite me to an evening service, I was still practicing. When she came into the family room to speak to me, I was a little annoyed, but politely let her speak. But this time, after declining again, she said, "The speaker thinks Jesus will return either this September or next September."

I didn't know anything about the rapture of the church. The second coming was somewhat familiar to me. Therefore, I thought she was referring to that event. Anyway, it piqued my interest, to say the least. My response was, "What time does church start"?

There was no way I was going to miss that. Donna was working the night shift again and didn't know anything about this.

The speaker was an evangelist who had written a book on Bible prophecy. His theory, based on Old and New Testament prophecies, pertained to when the rapture may occur. It sounded credible to me, mainly because I knew nothing of the subject. Obviously, his time of the rapture was not correct. However, his end-times prophetic reasoning was correct; almost all have come true except the rapture.

Sometime during his message, something amazing happened—I knew that Jesus Christ was God. This was the second time in my life that I actually came to that conclusion. The first time was when I attended a kindergarten Sunday-school class. I remember saying to my five-year old self, "I believe Jesus is God." Where that came from is only conjecture, but from that time until eighth grade, I liked learning about Jesus. In fact, friends called me "deacon" then.

My remembrance of that was suddenly interrupted when I heard the evangelist pose, "Wouldn't it be nice if when the trumpet sounds at Rosh Hashanah, September 6th, Jesus would return for His church?" Rosh Hashanah is the Jewish New Year. The evangelist had said, "The year 1975, in Hebrew, spells out the word 'Shilo,' which means the Messiah." That got my attention, but for a different reason. My Birthday was September 6.

The same thought, Jesus is God, just as it had that day in the kindergarten Sunday-school class, came to mind that night. However, this time, I definitely knew it was true.

Back in kindergarten, I was happy to know that. However, this night, I didn't know how to feel. My fear was that my past sins may have prohibited any chance of personal redemption.

I told the evangelist about my birthday being September 6. He replied with an early, "Happy birthday!" He didn't know that I wasn't saved yet, and neither did I. In fact, I hadn't even known what being saved meant.

Jesus Christ was, is, and always will be God's Son, the second person of the triune God. Fulfilled prophecy and its importance to belief in Jesus was new to me. Upon hearing the evangelist relate one fulfilled prophecy after another, I was struck with the fact that when God says something is going to happen, it happens. The fact that the rapture hadn't happened on my birthday didn't really bother me. No one knows the day or the hour, only the Father knows. I was unaware of that then, but not for long. The evangelist's error was using man's logic to replace God's will. If we aren't to know it, forget it. The whole world will know when it happens.

While listening to his message, my mind had this one recurring thought: I had sinned too much for God to want me. Sound familiar? If true, it was too late for me to be saved. In sharing that with my neighbors after the service, they quickly responded:

"For the wages of sin is death, but the free gift of God is eternal life in Jesus Christ our Lord." (Romans 3:23 ESV)

Salvation is a gift? No one earns a gift! It's either received or rejected. I was catching on, maybe there was hope for me yet.

Before that night, I used to argue against the Bible. As many do without having read the Bible, I would launch into my philosophy of life. Whatever that was, it included my made-up god. However, upon hearing that verse, I decided it may be a good idea for me to start reading God's Word. My neighbors gave me an old King James Version (KJV), which I appreciated.

My first task was to read the New Testament. The neighbors told me to start with the Gospel of John. Having learned the sequence of the books of the New Testament in fourth grade, I actually knew where to find it.

For the first time in my life, Scripture began to make sense. I had never been able to understand the Bible, but that night, I did. It excited me, which was also a first. While reading, I continued to struggle with my former sins. All at once, the peace of God, which truly does surpass all understanding, came over me. What an overwhelming feeling that was. Thankfully, the Lord continued to comfort me as I read.

There's a funny side note to this. Donna and I had agreed to be cremated when we pass. Somehow, in the course of the conversation at the neighbor's home, the subject arose. They told me to hold off on that because they were taught that Christians should be buried. I thought of that while I was reading. I quickly stopped to write a note to Donna, who was still at work. It read:

"I went to church tonight and now believe that Jesus Christ is God! If I should die before you come home, don't cremate me. Otherwise, I'll explain later."

Thinking back on that ridiculous note, it must have been both the most startling and most welcome note my wife ever received from me. She always hoped that we would go to some church, any church, as a family. If she had been praying about that, the Lord definitely heard.

That must have been the moment that I became a believer, saved by grace through faith alone. However, I didn't think of it that way yet and, therefore, didn't know it. I just believed.

But I had to have received the Holy Spirit that night because of what followed the next day.

I began to witness what the evangelist had said. In Acts 1:8, Jesus tells the Apostles, his disciples and all believers how we can know that we have received the Holy Spirit.

Jesus stated, *"But you shall receive power when the Holy Spirit has come upon you, and you shall be witnesses to me in Jerusalem, and in all Judea and Samaria, and to the end of the earth."* (Acts 1:8 NKJV)

Therefore, the proof of the indwelling of the Holy Spirit in a believer is the power to witness that Jesus is God and the only way to heaven. My knowledge was obviously limited, but I did it.

On the way to school with Gary the next morning, I explained the rapture as it was presented the previous evening. It never occurred to me that it may blow him away. He also heard of my rekindled belief that Jesus is indeed God. I don't remember his response. But during the ensuing trips to school in the mornings, he heard more. I continued to tell him what I was learning through my own Bible study, Sunday school, and church. I'm not sure he was happy about that, but he politely listened as he continued to accelerate.

As my trust in Christ grew, I continued to share my testimony with others. That included inviting others to our church, and, most of the time, they came. The church was growing as a result. Pastor Ron seemed very happy that I was attending and bringing friends. I too was grateful, if for no other reason than just hearing the Word taught correctly.

I didn't realize that Ron was waiting to hear that I had prayed to receive the Lord. I hadn't done that yet, I really didn't know it was expected. Remember, I didn't read the end of the tract. I should have. But the faith to believe in Jesus and His Word had filled my soul, and—I knew it!

"So then Faith comes by hearing, and hearing by the Word of God." (Romans 10:17 NKJV)

CHAPTER 36

Sealing the Deal

Once I reread the tract, the simple prayer was there. However, I didn't read it until after another really incredible event happened, possibly the most important event of my life.

Our Saturday morning jazz-piano class was interesting, as well as a wonderful learning experience. We also had a great teacher. The room was set up in such a way that two rows of studio electric pianos, placed back to back, stretched from the doorway of the long narrow classroom to the teacher's piano at the front. Studio pianos are similar to spinets, only with seventy-two keys instead of eighty-eight. They are not the folding, suitcase type, but are all one piece and can only be moved by rollers. The other feature was that the pianos had earphone jacks, by which we could freely practice individually before class without others hearing our mistakes.

One very sunny Saturday morning, I entered the classroom and sat down at my piano, still wearing my sunglasses. As I put on my headset, it occurred to me that I hadn't removed them. Usually, I would put them in my shirt pocket, but for some reason, that morning, I just set them on the top of the piano. While practicing, I noticed, from the vibration, that my sunglasses were about to drop between two pianos. Before I could reach them, they went over the edge.

A talented young pianist across from me peered down from her piano. She enthusiastically said, "Hey, your sunglasses are resting on a little book down there, maybe it's someone's little black book." For some reason, instead of pulling out her piano to retrieve them for me, she ran all the way around the line of pianos to mine. She pulled my piano out a little, reached down, and picked up both the sunglasses and the book—a little Gideon Bible.

Almighty God often uses Gideon Bibles, by themselves, to turn the hearts of sinners to His Son and His finished work on the cross. I heard a Gideon story once that blew me away. A rail commuter had thrown a Gideon Bible out of a train's bathroom window. The Bible hit a hobo sitting along the railroad's right-of-way. He recovered it and began reading. He found salvation explained within its pages and received Christ as his Savior and Lord that day. The Lord totally turned his life around. He went from being a beggar living off others to a citizen of the kingdom and taking his place in society.

That day in class, I was totally amazed. She gave my sunglasses to me and then looked at the book. When she finally realized what it was, she handed it to me and said, "Here, do you want to get saved?" It was at that moment that I fully understood what that term meant. I replied, "Yes, I do! Thanks." She looked at me, shrugged her shoulders, and said, "Huh!" To me, this discovery was too much for coincidence. Too many things that I couldn't explain had already taken place, but this was the event that finally sealed the deal.

With the little Bible, I drove home to see if it could answer one question. The kids were downstairs watching TV, and Donna needed to leave. I didn't tell her or the kids what had happened in class. I wanted to be by myself to talk with the Lord.

While sitting on my bed just staring at the Bible, the thought came, "There must be a reason for finding this Bible." Finally, I looked up and said, "Lord, I now know you are doing something in me, but were You the one who took drinking away from me?" The first rolled cigarette was in 1860 and they weren't manufactured in mass until the 1880s. Therefore, there was no need to include smoking in my prayer. However, there was beer, wine, and hard liquor all the way back to Noah, maybe even before Him. Therefore, I hoped to find the answer in His Word.

I randomly opened the Bible to **1 Thessalonians 5:5–9.** To my amazement, the verses read,

> *"For you are all sons of light and sons of day. We are not of night nor of darkness; so then let us not sleep as others do, **but let us be alert and sober.** For those who sleep do their sleeping at night, and those who get drunk get drunk at night. But since we are of the day, let us be sober, having put on the breastplate of faith and love, and as a helmet, the hope of salvation."* (1 Thessalonians 5:4-8 NASB)

But, it was verse 9 that really got to me:

> *"For God has not destined us for wrath, but for obtaining salvation through our Lord Jesus Christ, who died for us, so that whether we are awake or asleep, we will live together with Him. Therefore encourage one another and build up one another, just as you also are doing."* (1 Thessalonians 5:9-10 NASB)

As my eyes filled with tears, I told the Lord that, as a sinner, I could not save myself. I continued, "Lord, I am sorry for my sins, which I now know you have forgiven. I believe that You, Jesus, died for all my sins to give me eternal life with You. Please come into my heart as my own personal Savior and Lord. Make me the kind of person that you want me to be."

That prayer was very similar to the one in the tract that I hadn't finished earlier. Once I finally read the tract completely, there it was. I now understood! Later on, in His Word, Jesus explained the change in my heart with respect to redemption in this way:

"Two men went up to the temple to pray, one a Pharisee and the other a tax collector. The Pharisee stood and prayed thus with himself, 'God, I thank you that I am not like other men—extortioners, unjust, adulterers, or even as this tax collector. I fast twice a week; I give tithes

of all that I possess.' And the tax collector, standing afar off, would not so much as raise his eyes to heaven, but beat his breast, saying, 'God, be merciful to me a sinner! I tell you, this man went down to his house justified rather than the other; for everyone who exalts himself will be humbled, and he who humbles himself will be exalted.'" (Luke 18:10–14 KJV)

Everyone on earth needs Jesus. Jesus made his offer of salvation to everyone, but most have rejected it. Why? It's human pride! It keeps us from seeing that we are sinners and cannot save ourselves. Sadly, many still feel they are favored of God by comparing themselves to others less fortunate.

The Pharisee didn't see himself as a sinner, but the tax-collector did. He knew he was a sinner and needed mercy. When a person humbles himself before God this way, the faith to know that he needs a savior is given to him. The ability to believe in the Messiah who paid it all at the cross for our sins is included in that faith. For this man, it was to believe in the Messiah which was to come. For us, it is to believe in the Messiah that has come. Just as Jesus said of this man, once we know we are saved, we are then justified by faith alone.

It's important to understand exactly what the Lord meant by the word "justified." For this, we need to look at the tax-collector's state of mind. First, he was despised by the Jews. Tax-collectors, as a rule, stole from the Jews in amounts many times what their fellow citizens owed.

Many might say they had a good thing going. They wouldn't be hauled off to court because the Romans liked the money. That may be why the Pharisee thanked God for not making him like this despised man. Of course, we know he was more like the man he considered despised, but just didn't know it. Most of us were in that camp at one time, judging ourselves by the bad deeds of others. Our egos reigned supreme prior to facing the reality that we don't deserve heaven.

On the other hand, the tax-collector knew he had to repent and be forgiven. He told God that he knew he was a sinner. FYI: when praying, it's best to be honest with God. That set the stage for his request's fulfillment. The self-identified sinner asked for mercy, which he received.

"Not by works of righteousness which we have done, but according to His mercy He saved us." (Titus 3:5 KJV)

What is mercy? Mercy is not being given what we deserve. It never occurred to the Pharisee to repent. He didn't think of himself as a sinner at that point. If he died still believing that lie, he could never receive God's mercy. Scripture is clear on that.

There is a second component that goes hand-in-hand with mercy.

"For by grace you have been saved through faith, and that not of yourselves; it is the gift of God, not of works, lest anyone should boast." (Ephesians 2:8-9 NKJV)

Grace is giving us what we didn't deserve. It is contingent upon something called faith. The greatest gift from God is "faith." It's not something we conjure up; it's strictly from Him to us. What is its purpose? It's given to anyone who asks in order to believe in Jesus. At that point, belief in Jesus, God's Son and our Savior, happens. It is through faith alone upon which we can believe in Christ's finished work on the cross. It gives us both mercy and grace.

This principle is humbling, but awesome. We didn't get what we and everyone else deserves, but we did get what neither we nor anyone else deserves. That is called justification. Someone once explained the word "justified," in this way; it's—just-as-if-I'd never sinned. That is how God looks at all believers. Once in the fold, our relationship with Him is born and we are His forever.

However, for many, pride often keeps them from thinking that way. Surely, those of us, especially in America, who have so much more than the rest of the world, can understand this. We want to think we were born basically good and that God made us that way, evidenced by our worldly prosperity. However, that was the position of the Pharisee. The tax-collector, on the other hand, realized what others refuse to accept, we are all sinners. We must acknowledge this before our God and Father of our Lord Jesus Christ to receive His glorious grace. Remember this Bible principle:

"God resists the proud, but gives grace to the humble." (James 4:6 NKJV)

After thanking the Lord for drawing me to Himself in this unusual way, I gathered myself and began to think about the kids. Are they old enough to understand salvation? That seemed like the right thing to ponder. After all, it took me twenty-six years from that day in kindergarten to finally comprehend its true meaning.

I went downstairs to tell them what I had just done. I then asked if they, too, would like to invite Jesus into their hearts and receive His free gift of eternal life. Even if they were too young to fully understand this, I felt they should have the choice. After all, we had been attending church together every Sunday for six weeks. Perhaps they had heard it during that time.

They looked at each other for a moment, and then Tracee, the youngest, said, "Daddy, the first time you let us go to church with the neighbors, we also asked Jesus into our hearts. Our teacher asked if we had anyone we wanted to pray for. We said, 'Yes! We want our new daddy to stop smoking and drinking, and you haven't done it since that day.'" Oh, for the faith of little children! If only all adults had it. My question was answered both by Scripture and through the kids. That was the only confirmation I needed. Needless to say, I was totally blown away.

The Lord had done a miracle by answering the prayer of our two children. It had been the reason that they were always looking at me strangely. They wanted to be certain that I would never again smoke or drink, which, thankfully, never happened. It was no longer their concern.

God's plan for my salvation was as much for them as it was for me, and it came at just the right time. I thanked them for their prayer and was quick to say that the Lord had heard them. To this day, I am extremely grateful to Him for leading them to pray for me.

I am also grateful to them for being obedient to God, even if they weren't aware of it. My life-changing experience was truly a miracle. And just thinking about it still confirms his wondrous work in me. The Lord was calling me, which couldn't have been clearer than it was that day. The effect of this miracle would change us as a family for the rest of our lives.

It was the most wonderful day of my life. I now knew—He had truly sealed the deal.

"Do not grieve the Holy Spirit of God, by whom you were sealed for the day of redemption." (Ephesians 4:30 NKJV)

CHAPTER 37

My Wonderful Surprise

I left this personal miracle for last. In terms of most of the others, it is still fairly recent. Only the emboli attack and the new car miracle happened more recently. However, it is one that has brought me great joy.

Before going on to relate this miracle, a short explanation of my relationship with the Lord is necessary. I relate to the Apostle Paul as the chief of sinners. I did a despicable thing while in the service. It resulted in a family previously unknown to me. Over seven years ago, I found out that I had a son and four wonderful but quite different grandchildren, all of whom I love dearly. It's a shame that I was not there for my son or his mother, but I have to live with that.

Growing up, I knew about Jesus and believed he was God, but I didn't know Him personally. Let me explain that. As a baseball lover growing up, my idol was Roberto Clemente. I never missed a box score during his seventeen-year career. He was incredible in every way. I loved Roberto Clemente even more than Ralph Kiner before him or Willie Stargell after him. There was no one like him, before or after, he was unique. Pittsburghers that saw him play would confirm that.

On New Year's Day 1973, at the age of thirty-seven, Roberto Clemente tragically died. In trying to get aid to the victims of the Nicaragua earthquake, his plane went down in the Caribbean Sea. His body was never found. I was crushed. It was hard to teach that week or do anything.

However, one day, in writing what I knew about him, something suddenly hit me—I never met him. I only knew of him, He did not know me. He had no relationship with me. If I had met him and asked him for something, he may have said, "Depart from me, I don't know you."

When applying that to God, a profound principle emerges. It's not enough to only know about Jesus, we need to have a genuine relationship with Him. I didn't have that then. If I had died early, God would have said, *"And then I will declare to them, 'I never knew you; depart from Me, you who practice lawlessness!'"* (Matthew 7:23 NKJV)

My salvation had depended on only what I heard of God in my church, but not really knowing God. I had no relationship with Him. Yet Jesus clearly said, *"And I, if I am lifted up from the earth, will draw all peoples to Myself"* (John 12:32 NKJV)

That was His promise to everyone, and thankfully, he kept it with me. I believe He keeps it with everyone, but sometimes, religion, pride, and many other things get in between Jesus and us.

Sometimes we feel confident that our good works outweigh our bad. If we are self-satisfied, we may not sense His draw at all. I can relate to that. Therefore, I didn't seek Him.

In actuality, no one seeks God. However, at a low point in life, I realized I was a sinner and could not save myself. That was the first step for me, which occurred seven years after I met a person named Gloria.

Regrettably, when I learned of her pregnancy, I didn't believe that it was my child. There were no DNA tests in those days. It was all about me then, God wasn't a consideration. Obviously, Gloria wasn't either. That totally immoral decision led me in a different spiritual direction. It was as if I was trying to clear my conscience by doing whatever looked or felt good. Many people have tried the same and found it doesn't work.

However, her child, a boy, whom she named David, was definitely mine. God reunited us, in His time, with perhaps the most wonderful miracle of my recent life. As a born-again Christian, I take full responsibility for my sinful actions in my darker days. However, there is no way that I can fully repay what David or his mother deserves. Even if I had the means to do it, it would not erase the damage I caused.

Does that mean David was a mistake? No! God knew him as He knew me and everyone else before the world began. I sinned, David didn't. The only mistakes were mine, especially in not taking responsibility for being his father. That compounded my sin.

I am eternally grateful to Gloria for raising him instead of putting him up for adoption. She was then and is now one of the nicest and finest women I have ever met. I have a lot of respect for her, and believe it or not, she and her husband are now good friends of ours.

It was David's mother who found me, but it was clearly God's doing. Seven years after he was born, while I was still on my knees praying to receive the Lord, something happened. God let me know, through an impression afterward, that I had a child out there. Trying to find Gloria proved useless. Her first name was in my memory, but not her last. After confessing my sin to the Lord, I hoped He would send my offspring to me when the time came.

Praying for David's mother came easily. It was finally obvious that she had been telling the truth. Unfortunately, I couldn't get too far with just her first name. It was my intention to find her, but how to do it eluded me. Her last name was a long one, which I finally saw in print, a little over seven years ago.

Of course, it was up to the Lord in His timing to bring about this miracle. I knew in my heart she had been truthful when she originally called me in the late '60s, but I didn't want to believe it then. The day I came to Christ, I did want to believe it. That's the type of effect a relationship with Jesus has on believers. The miracle is the way it came about. Gloria was trying to find me! However, something happened to make me want to find her.

One day, my cousin Crissy got an "I Finally Found You" email. It was from her son Jim, whom she had put up for adoption. She made contact with him and was encouraged that he was happy to have found her. Then she called me to ask if I would meet with him. Since we lived in an area close to his, it was easy to oblige. Chrissy was several states away, and, therefore, I was happy to do it.

She came to Pittsburgh to meet him. My cousin and her son, Jim, were finally together after forty-five years. My wife, Crissy, Jim, and I attended a Pirates' game that night. During the game, she was smiling ear-to-ear. When her son had noticed that, he looked over at her and said, "I've never seen anyone so happy in my entire life."

My sister Judy had been praying for our cousin's son to be restored to our family. Once she knew he was found, her comment was, "Well, it's about time he turned up!"

God had answered Judy's prayer as well as Crissy's. My cousin's miracle got me to asking the Lord, "When am I going to meet my own son or daughter?" The Lord answered my prayer in an awesome way, which comes next. Suffice it to say—what a wonderful surprise!

"this was the LORD's doing, And it is marvelous in our eyes" (Mark 12:11 (NKJV)

CHAPTER 38

Making Beauty from Ashes

Several days after my cousin returned to Chicago, Sherri went to California for a family visit. While alone, I began to feel a little sad that my prayer hadn't been answered. I was still certain that my son or daughter was out there. Sitting at my desk in my home office one morning, I asked the Lord to restore my offspring to me.

The next morning, a radio commercial for mylife.com awakened me. I didn't think too much about it until I sat down to breakfast. The same commercial aired also on TV. When I went into my office and turned on my computer, there was the same ad for the same site. It was then that I thought, maybe the Lord is trying to get my attention.

After entering the site, I filled out the requested information, which prompted a pop-up window. It pointed to three women who were trying to find me. Payment was required to enter the site to find out who the women were. Paying for websites never sits well with me. As I was considering that, the window changed. A fourth woman was added that very moment. That startled me into paying for the site to see who they were.

But before entering it, I said to the Lord, "If one of the women is Gloria from Buffalo, I'll know this was from You." Two of the women listed were actually the same person who was looking for a high-school friend with whom she had graduated in Florida. The fourth one, who appeared as I was considering the site, was my dear sister in Minnesota.

When I talked to her about it, she said, "I just wanted to see if it would work." Apparently, the Lord had also spoken to her heart, but she didn't know it. Think about that! What are the odds that my sister would have such a curious urge to get into a website at almost the exact same time I was considering paying for it?

The third person was Gloria from Buffalo. By this time, I wasn't surprised. The way things were going, I knew her name would be there. Her age was listed as two years younger than mine. It was definitely Gloria, and I knew it. After being blown away by the three invitations to join the site, I paid to join and there she was. Obviously, it was the Lord's doing!

The next thing to consider was her family associations. There were several men, one of whom was David. He had her maiden name, which I finally remembered. Therefore, I assumed him to be my son. However, in trying to find Gloria's phone number, I totally struck out.

To say I was excited would be an understatement. It should have occurred to me that she was married, but it didn't. The entire event excited me so much, I wasn't thinking straight. Her husband's name was there as an association, but somehow, I didn't put two and two together. David's last name was the one that I recognized. Being somewhat frustrated (meaning I didn't want to make a mistake), I called my cousin. She had done a ton of genealogy work for my mother's side of the family. Cris had found people and phone numbers from all over the country and world. I hoped she could do the same for me, and she did.

First, she realized that Gloria's last name was her married name and that her husband was the other man listed as an associate. I failed at trying to get Gloria's number, but my cousin succeeded with his. Once she had it figured out, Cris called Gloria. When she got her voice mail, she stated her name and number. She then explained that she does genealogical work and left this message: "I'd like to know if you know a John Corfield. If you do, please give me a call, if not, forget it."

A few days later, as I was about to fly to Memphis, Tennessee, for a speaking engagement, Cris called. She said, "I just got off the phone with Gloria. She may be the nicest person to whom I've ever spoken [that's Gloria]. She wants you to call her tomorrow morning around ten o'clock."

Sleep never came to me that night. What should be said when she answers? Losing sleep didn't help my speech either the following evening, but we got through it. At exactly 10:00 AM in the morning, the call was made as requested. When she answered, this is how it went:

Me: Hi Gloria, this is John Corfield.
Gloria: John, how are you? (She said enthusiastically.)

That really stunned me. At this point, I was expecting a hand to come out of the phone to slap me across the face several times, to which I would have said, "You missed a spot." I deserved a lot more than that.

Me: I'm fine, Gloria, how are you?
Gloria: I'm also fine.
Me: Just to make sure I'm talking to the right person, we met—
Gloria: When you were in the Honor Guard in Washington, DC.
Me: And you called me to say I was going to be a father sometime in October?
Gloria: Yes, that's right.
Me: Is David my son?
Gloria: He is.
Me: Then, Gloria, I owe you a huge apology, what I did was . . .

I was about to say despicable when she cut me off. What she said next blew me away, to say the least.

Gloria: John, stop! I am a Christian now and I have forgiven you of EVERYTHING! And, I hope you've forgiven me.

Me: I don't have anything to forgive you for, it was my
fault. I walked away.

Gloria: I used to be bitter about it, but not anymore. I am
happily married, and I hope you are too.

Me: I am happily married, Gloria, but what I did was
totally wrong, and I'm very ashamed of it. There's
not much I can do about it now, but it was despicable. I have to live with it, but I am really sorry for
what it cost you.

Gloria: By the way, we have four grandchildren.

I hadn't even thought of that, but I was really interested when
she said it. After telling her why I was in Tennessee, I also mentioned
my lack of sleep that night, to which she responded, "I didn't sleep
either."

To be forgiven of everything by Gloria brought home a new
meaning of grace. I deserved nothing from her but ridicule and
repugnance. I messed up her life. She deserved much better, and yet
she was forgiving me and wanted me to forgive her? What an incredible woman. Only God could give someone a heart like hers.

Gloria didn't marry until David was twenty-two years old. Her
parents had helped her raise our son. Sadly, both of them have since
passed away.

I had never had a negative thought about her in any way, which
I conveyed to her. I also said, "The day I received Christ as my Savior
and Lord, I knew you had been telling the truth." I let her know that
I hoped to contact her earlier but couldn't remember her last name.

The irony in this is that I lived in Rochester, New York, for a
year, only about sixty miles from where they resided. I often think
about what she went through to raise David and what David missed
by my not being there for both of them. I regret that, but again, I
have to live with it.

That is not to say that I regret marrying Donna and raising our
kids. What happened didn't take the Lord by surprise. My belief is
that He orchestrated our marriage. Troy and Tracee needed a full-
time father, and I obviously needed them, as demonstrated in my

testimony. I am a Christian because of them, something for which I am eternally grateful.

My concern was David not knowing our family medical history, which she agreed was also their concern. Some of our family's medical history is serious. Therefore, I went on to list the various medical conditions, which David needed to know. I also left the list with Gloria in case David didn't want me to contact him.

In my joy, I couldn't wait to share this with my family. My offspring David, my son, had finally been found! This miracle demonstrates just how much God loves us. When we finally ended the call, I felt a lot better. What a huge lesson in God's grace. He was—**making beauty from ashes**.

"He will give a crown of beauty for ashes, a joyous blessing instead of mourning." (Isaiah 61:3 NLT)

CHAPTER 39

Grace upon Grace

"Noah found grace in the eyes of the Lord." (Genesis 6:8 NKJV)

G loria said later that she worked for a company that let her use their computer for personal use. She registered with mylife.com to research me, hoping to find a picture of my kids to see if they looked like David or me. She couldn't find pictures of the kids anywhere, just one of me. Later, she would find out through David that my children were adopted. David kept tabs on me for several years after that but didn't contact me. He said he didn't want to interrupt my life.

Gloria told me that David was an attorney and that he had graduated from Notre Dame Law School. She added, "John, we didn't have a dummy." It was appreciated that she looked at it that way, but it was a hard for me to totally accept the word "we."

Before we hung up, I asked Gloria for permission to call David. She enthusiastically replied, "He would like to hear from you." That excited me! I couldn't wait to talk with my son, but getting through was not the easiest thing to do. After leaving many messages without success, I decided to leave the medical history on my next message. After doing so, I added that I loved him and have ever since 1975 when the Lord let me know somehow that I had a child.

A reply to that message came very quickly. David said he was in court but asked me to call him that evening. It was an incredible conversation. After explaining the medical history once more, we talked a little about his life. I told him how great it was to talk with him. At that point, he asked whether I had something else to do. I replied that I didn't. Then he asked, "Would you mind if we kept talking for a while?"

I said, "Not at all!" It became clear that he wanted to talk with me as much as I wanted to talk with him. That call lasted for hours. What a joy it was to finally have a conversation with the son I had loved all of those years without ever knowing or meeting him.

The next day, I told both my sisters about David and what had transpired between us. One of my sisters was incredibly supportive, encouraging me in every way. The other was not as happy about it. Although, not understanding the role the Lord God gave her to play in this miracle, she wanted to see pictures of David and his family.

She had done a lot for me in my life, and, therefore, her wishes were to be respected. David sent the pictures from his birth to the present and current pictures of his family. That was enough for me, but not enough for her. She noticed that David didn't look like me at all. That was true eight years ago, maybe, but I wouldn't be surprised if that doesn't happen later, as it did with my father and me. In fact, I am beginning to see it in David.

I told her to look at the picture of my grandson, Andrew. He looked very much like my eighth-grade picture. Coincidentally, he had just entered the eighth grade. Nevertheless, my sister insisted on a DNA test. It would certify whether I was or was not his father.

The feeling that came over me the day of my conversion and its fulfillment was enough for me. However, it was also owed to my wife and extended family to get it done. It was a good idea to have the proof for everyone in both families. In fact, after bringing it up to David, he not only agreed but also said that Gloria wanted us to do it. That told me what to expect from the result of the test, but I still did it for the others.

The DNA kit arrived fairly quickly, which we appreciated. The two of us were eager to meet each other. Therefore, we arranged a visit soon after receiving the kit. We decided to do the swabs together the next day after meeting. I would then drive the sealed envelope to the lab in Cincinnati. He was fine with that.

In starting out the next day to meet my new family, it occurred to me that I hadn't called Troy or Tracee. I didn't remember that they had been told of this possibility.

As is common today, I left a message for both. My son Troy replied first. He said, "Way to go, Dad." I was very happy to hear him say that. I wasn't sure how he would feel about it later, but that day, he was very supportive.

I didn't know what my daughter, Tracee, would say. When she called, I explained the story again. While doing that, I could hear her crying in the background. Several thoughts went through my mind. Had I offended her? Had I blown her image of me as her father? Apparently, my thoughts were way off base.

When I asked her what was wrong, her reply blew me away. She said, "Dad, you told us that story when we were in high school. Ever since that day, I've been praying that you would find your son or daughter, and it finally happened. I am really happy for you!"

In a way, that may have brought Tracee and me closer together. I really appreciated what she said and how she felt about it. God had answered both of our prayers. What a wonderful day that was.

God was adding to me—**grace upon grace.**

"From His fullness we have all received grace upon grace." (John 1:16 Berean Study Bible)

CHAPTER 40

My Cup Runneth Over

With the moral support from Troy and Tracee, I went on to meet David and his talented wife, Beth. For many years, she had been encouraging David to contact me. However, he didn't want to interrupt my life. I know how that feels. Prior to my Christian walk, I debated the right to interrupt my offspring's life, if one existed. However, my conversion changed that. When the opportunity came up, I took the risk. I'm very happy with the result.

We first met at my hotel parking lot. He brought my eighth-grade grandson Andrew with him. We then went to the high school to meet Beth and my sixth-grade granddaughter, Katie. I had to wait to meet Mary; she was still an infant, not even a one-year-old yet. Once we met, I knew she was special.

Of course, all of the kids are special to me in their own way, but I knew Mary would be the one to work the room when friends and family would visit. I wasn't wrong in that initial feeling. If there is anyone that can entertain, it's Mary!

I wanted desperately to be their friend, but it turned out better than that. I became part of their family very quickly that night. I had decided earlier that they were already part of mine.

David and I went to dinner together at one of his favorite restaurants. It was a great way to get to know each other. After dinner, we went to see my grandson, Matthew, play basketball for his high school. I cannot express the joy of seeing that. He hadn't been playing basketball very long, but he did well. He was aggressive on defense, with rebounds and steals and adequate on offense. So many emotions were going through my mind. At that moment, I would have loved to have been his coach.

We went back to the house for the rest of the evening. On the way there, David had warned me that Matt didn't feel comfortable with my visit. But Matt never showed it; in fact, he talked with me more than the others did. When I was ready to leave, he may have been the first one to hug me and call me Grandpa, which he has been doing ever since. I told my new family I loved them and was very happy to finally meet them.

It was not possible to see them the next day. I felt a little bad about that. Being with them the night before was really enjoyable. But David and I still had to do the test before I left. When he came to my hotel, he mentioned to the desk clerk that he was there to meet his father and gave her my name. The desk clerk said that when she saw him, she knew who his father was. When I showed up down-stairs, she said, "There he is."

I could see that it made David feel good that someone outside the family noticed a resemblance. I could see the resemblance to my father around his eyes, but apparently, I was the only one in my family who could.

We went to my room to do the swabs and seal them in the envelope. Earlier, it had occurred to me that he and/or Beth may see a risk of allowing me to leave with the swabs. She may have feared a swab switch on the way to the Cincinnati lab. David never mentioned that or he would have insisted that I mail it. His trust in me was encouraging. However, wives are generally not as trusting, which I totally understand.

It probably wouldn't have been the first time someone did that. Beth had asked a few times why we didn't want to mail it. While waiting for David, I realized then that the idea may be weighing heavily on her heart.

As a saved and committed follower of Jesus Christ, I would never do it, but how could she know that? Later, it was disclosed that Beth was afraid of a transfer of swabs for good reason.

Beth didn't know me and didn't realize how much a positive test meant to me. It would prove what I already knew the day I prayed to receive Christ. I had loved David for many years prior to finding him, and now I loved the entire family.

Before we did the swabs, I gave David a book that had been very influential to my early growth as a Christian. It was Josh McDowell's *New Evidence that Demands a Verdict*. I thought an attorney would really enjoy reading it. I suggested he check out the prophecy evidence and the C.S. Lewis chapter, "Jesus Christ: Lord, Liar, or Lunatic." Later, David told me that he was all over the book, which pleased me very much.

We said our goodbyes, which were difficult, but I was really excited to get on to the lab. Unfortunately, I never envisioned the inclement weather ahead. Rain caused a lot of accidents on the way to Cincinnati. Traffic was held up several times, impeding my progress. Two car accidents tied up traffic. Fortunately, I arrived at the scenes just after they happened. Though I was frustrated, the conditions of the drivers and passengers were obviously more important.

After being allowed to pass the second accident, my concern was that I wouldn't make it in time. Siri was a bit confused upon my arrival in the area. She had me turn the wrong way on the right road. I called the clinic to tell them I was close but needed their help with directions, which they supplied. No matter how bad the weather was, I was intent on getting there before their 5:00 PM closing.

Upon arrival, they too asked me why we hadn't just mailed it. Apparently, they had the same concern. I told them how important it was for us to have results by Friday morning and why. I told them the entire story, which appeared to touch their hearts. They assured me that they would get it done by then, and they did.

David and I both received the results, but I wasn't aware of that. After reading the results, I forwarded the information to him in case he didn't get the report. The results were 99.9998% that I was David's father. The last sentence in the report said, "This man cannot be excused from being the father." No kidding! Perhaps they had to say that in case a lawsuit might be brought against me. To me, those conclusive words were wonderful.

I was ecstatic with the results. After the test confirmed me as David's father, Beth said she had been thinking of sending me a cigar and a card that said, "Congratulations, it's a boy!"

David, Beth, Gloria, and her husband, Vic, and my four grandchildren have been a huge blessing to me. My little, now eight-year-old granddaughter, Mary, will never know anything other than I am her Grandpa John.

My oldest grandson, Matthew, keeps in touch with me by phone. I was able to see him play football the following fall. Every now and then, he calls me and we have a good talk.

Andrew, my other grandson, has not kept in touch, but we have had some good conversations when we've been together. Andrew is probably a genius, but he doesn't know it yet. I feel very positive that he will land on his feet someday.

When I was young, I loved to climb trees, which I had mentioned to Andrew. During the next visit, he walked barefoot out to the big tree in the backyard, jumped up, and grabbed two branches. He quickly pulled his body up into the tree and onto another branch. It was what I loved to do, with the exception of the bare feet.

The person I became the closest to early on was my granddaughter Katie, now Kate. She initiated it by texting me after our family reunion. Her message went right to my heart.

Of course, being technically challenged, as are many of my age, she had to teach me how to text. We've stayed in touch that way now for seven years. She graduated from high school with many accolades.

Kate was a member of The National Honor Society and other academic and community service clubs. She not only graduated in the top ten of her high school class of 325 but was also the commencement speaker. Kate received a full ride as an honors student to Purdue. Her major is Biology to prepare her for medical school.

Kate was also a cheerleader, a diver on the swim team, and a singles tennis player. She is a natural athlete, as is her mother. She loves to compete, as did her grandfather John (yours truly). She has accomplished more in scholastics than I ever did. But there's no need to talk about my grade point average in high school. Let's just say I was a late bloomer and leave it at that.

The two boys have abilities but will also be late-bloomers. Unfortunately, I see some of my good and bad traits in both. What matters is that I love them very much and I'm counting on the Lord to bring both of them into a relationship with Him. Hopefully, they will discover and use the gifts He has given them to His glory. I don't doubt that He will do that, but it may be awhile.

The summer after David and I had discovered one another, we had a family reunion at our house in Cranberry Township, Pennsylvania. It was held to honor both my new family and my cousin's newfound son. My cousin, the family historian on my mother's side, told all of us some interesting things about our relatives. The biggest surprise was finding out that we are related to Queen Elizabeth, although very distantly. That was news to me and to the rest of the family. I knew David and family enjoyed hearing that.

Then there was the belated thrill of throwing a baseball with my son David and grandson Matthew. I loved teaching sports to my son, Troy, who turned out to be a really good athlete. Unfortunately, David missed that, but he did play soccer in high school.

I shared the greatest part of this God story with everyone after dinner. Yes, God had saved me by grace through the faith Jesus gave me to believe. I understood that. But out of all of the miracles I've related in this book, it was through Gloria and David that I truly came to understand, in a refreshing way, God's amazing grace.

The fact that Gloria, a born-again Christian, was no longer bitter toward me, but rather had forgiven me of everything, is the personification of grace. That she has accepted me as part of her family is the miracle of miracles. That David, who had every right to be bitter with me, still welcomed me into his family. Though it was definitely undeserved, it meant everything to me and still does.

That's what the grace of God is. Jesus paid sin's debt to give eternal life to all who would believe. In every way, it is the perfect example of God's grace to us in sending Christ to die in our place.

Jesus had to do it because none of us could ever do anything to erase the havoc sin has wreaked in many lives. If it weren't for Gloria's devotion to God, David could have ended up as many abandoned kids have, in deep trouble. Having taught students in that terrible position, I know how his story could have ended, but thankfully didn't.

In thinking about my undeserved gift from the Lord, I thought of this verse:

> *Every good gift and perfect gift is from above,*
> *and comes down from the Father of lights, with*
> *whom there is no variation or shadow of turning.*
> (James 1:17 NKJV)

From the entire experience of God's miracles in my life, my testimony, God's hole-in-one for Gary's benefit, and all the rest, it was finding David which brought all the joy a person could want. The expanded meaning of God's grace will never be forgotten. Simply put—my cup runneth over. Amen and Amen!

> *"You anointest my head with oil, my cup*
> *runneth over."* (Psalm 23:5 KJV)

CHAPTER 41

The Shema

A few months after my conversion, I met with the pastor of the Canyon Community Church. Pastor Ed, a Jewish convert to Christianity, was a tremendous help to me as a young believer. Most converted Jews consider themselves Jews by birth but Christians by the second birth, which is our spiritual birth through the Holy Spirit by faith alone.

I was fascinated by what he showed me from the Old Testament. He took me to Genesis first to show me the trinity, or triune God. Most would find that interesting since neither word can be found in either testament. But it's there, written differently, but meaning the same thing.

This is what I learned from Pastor Ed. In the first three verses of the Bible, we see God the Father, God the Holy Spirit, and God the Son. The Father, in verse 1, is introduced as the Master Planner of creation. The Holy Spirit, which is everywhere, hovered over the earth when it was formless and void. In verse 3, we see the Light of the World, Jesus Christ, who illuminated everything for creation as He spoke it into existence. As the Apostle John said, Jesus created everything. Of course, I mentioned this earlier, but it is always good to review:

"All things were made through Him, and without Him nothing was made that was made." (John 1:3 NKJV)

"Let us make man in our image." (Genesis 1:26 KJV) What did God mean by "our image?" And to whom was He speaking?

"I will be his Father, and he shall be My son. If he commits iniquity, I will chasten him with the rod of men and with the blows of the sons of men." (2 Samuel 7:14 NKJV)

God the Father was talking to Jesus and the Holy Spirit. We know He wasn't speaking to the angels because they were created by God. We also know from the book of Hebrews: *For to which of the angels did he ever say:*

> *"You are my Son Today I have begotten You?"*
> *And, again: "I will be to Him a Father, And He*
> *shall be to me a Son?"* (Hebrews 1:5 NKJV)

The answer is clearly none. Since angels were not created in God's image, the Father had to be speaking to the other two persons of the trinity, both totally God. This is the first clue that there is one God in three persons. The Father had to be speaking with the Holy Spirit and the eternal King, the promised Messiah, His Son, Jesus the Christ, Our Savior and Lord. Remember, Jesus is totally God and totally man. Therefore, Man is created in His image.

You may ask, "How can God be in three persons?" That's a great question! Pastor Ed solved it for me. The answer is found by two words in the Shema, the most important tenet in Judaism. It is a prayer and a command to be recited daily. Shema is the Hebrew word that means and commands "hear," and it is the first word of the verse, which begins in Deuteronomy 6:4:

"Hear O Israel, the Lord our God is one LORD." (KJV)

Most translations also render "the Lord is one." Several others finish with "alone." Many misinterpret that as meaning only the Father is truly God. However, in Hebrew, the word used for an absolute one is "yachid," which does not appear in the Shema. An example of that would be, I'm holding up my index finger. The answer is yachid. It means there is absolutely only one index finger.

However, in the Shema, the word used for "one" is "Echod." It's a composite "one." An example of Echod would be five fingers make up one hand. In this case, it's Father, Son, and Holy Spirit make up One God.

There is more evidence of a triune God. "Elohim" is the most commonly used word for God in Scripture, and it's also a plural. It means three degrees of personality. It confirms the first three verses of Genesis, which point out the three personalities of the Godhead. That nails it!

However, there is still more evidence in the Old Testament. Pastor Ed continued by taking me to another verse. The writer of Proverbs, asks. *"Who hath ascended up into heaven, or descended? who hath gathered the wind in his fists? who hath bound the waters in a garment? who hath established all the ends of the earth? what is his name, and what is his son's name, if thou canst tell?"* (Proverbs 30:4 KJV)

Remember, the Old Testament Psalms and Proverbs were written one thousand years before Jesus appeared as a man. Psalm 22 describes the crucifixion of God's Holy one, nine hundred years before crucifixion became the Roman Empire's mode of capital punishment. Isaiah 53 describes the reason for his death on our behalf. It was written 750 years before Christ. Both of these passages talk about the Messiah and his finished work on the cross.

The only one who could have fulfilled those prophecies was, in Hebrew "Yeshua," or Jesus—the Christ. "Christ" is the Greek word for the Hebrew word "Messiah." Yeshua means "Savior," which is the same thing. Therefore, we can see that the Old Testament does tell us that Jesus is God, the second person of the trinity. Not only that, He is also God's anointed one, the prophesied Messiah, our Savior and Lord.

Jesus said, "but if I do, though you do not believe Me, believe the works, that you may know and believe that the Father is in Me, and I in Him." (John 10:38 NKJV)

The totally man and totally God Jesus did the miraculous works of His Father, as prophesied, before the cross and afterward. His works after His ascension have all been done through Christians in some way. Since His resurrection, His works—through His followers—have been witnessed by many believers and nonbelievers for almost two thousand years.

Many of the miracles the Lord did, through me, happened during the first three years of my walk with Him. I suspect that the

Lord wanted me to be sold out to Him in my faith. He knew I would need to be in order to endure the eighteen-year illness of my deceased wife, Donna.

It is my belief that because we are in an age of chaotic uncertainty, He also planned for me to share the miracles contained in this book.

Understanding the Shema is essential to understanding the nature of God and his plan for salvation. However, isn't it odd that today's Jews start their prayers every day with the Shema, but do not realize the composite word for one, Echod, is the word used to describe the triune God? They also may not know that the most common name for the God in the Old Testament, Elohim, means God in three degrees of personality. Therefore, the Echod Elohim make up the one and only true God. The good news, according to Bible prophecy, is this: one day they will recognize that fact when they see Jesus return to save the remnant of Israel and other nations.

I thank God for Pastor Ed who showed me this evidence. Since the evidence of both is contained in that prayer, we praise the Lord for giving us—the Shema.

"Hear O Israel, the Lord our God is One LORD."
(Deuteronomy 6:4 KJV)

Summary

CHAPTER 42

The Biggest Decision One Could Make

Miracles are fascinating, especially when one is a part of them in some way. God is still working miracles to draw those He loves, which is everyone. The Scripture says that He hated Esau but loved Jacob. However, the Lord was talking about the character of each. He loves everyone, but not everyone's character. Bad character can change, if its owner receives Christ as his Savior and Lord. Sadly, not everyone will receive Him, regardless of character. In fact, most will reject Him. However, those that receive Him will live with Him forever. Those who receive Him have the faith of Jacob. Those who reject Him are as faithless as Esau. They depend totally on themselves and not on God for everything.

Not all born-again Christians need a miracle like mine to get their attention, but all will experience some type of miracle at some point. It happens usually after one realizes that he is a sinner in need of the Savior and, therefore, must make a decision. Salvation comes with the gift of faith from our Lord. That is the best miracle of our lives, if we act upon it. Once we receive Jesus, our lives take on a purpose. It's often one that we've never considered. Accepting His offer of salvation by grace through faith is the biggest and best decision anyone can make.

All the giants of the faith were self-confessed sinners just as we are, but they still preached the gospel to everyone they could. They weren't doing it to score points for their own salvation. They did it to glorify God through the salvation of others. All believers are to do the same!

Therefore, my hope for all who read this God story will also commit their lives to Christ. To those who haven't done it yet, He's waiting for you to come to Him. If you want the faith to believe—all you have to do is ask.

It will not hurt you to surrender your life to Christ in any way. It is not against any denominational doctrine. In fact, it will make you a better church member. I've heard people ask, "By praying to receive Christ, can I still be a [fill in the denomination]?" Yes, you can still belong to your denomination if you want. It will make serving God in your church more meaningful.

However, if you truly follow God, He may lead you in a different direction. With me, He led me to a Bible-believing church. Whatever your denominational preference, your pastor should be teaching and preaching salvation through faith alone. If you belong to a church that only liturgically recognizes God's Word but it's never referred to in the sermons, you may want more. If you want God's Word, there are many churches today that emphasize and teach God's Word.

I know how important the Bible is for your own spiritual growth. It's not only the mind of Christ, the Word is Christ. (John 1:1 KJV) You will miss a lot of what God wants for you if you remain a baby Christian the rest of your life.

In this life, we are being tested to determine whether or not we truly want to be with God forever. Those who want to live with Our Savior and Lord, Jesus Christ, must surrender their lives honestly and humbly to Him.

He seeks a personal relationship with each human being, and He has been building those relationships, one person at a time for two thousand years. He died for it and rose again to make it available to all who would believe by faith alone. By now, the reader realizes how important the basic doctrine of faith in Christ alone is. It cannot be over stressed.

Therefore, if you, the reader, desire to have a relationship with Christ, first, ask Jesus for the faith to believe in His finished work on the cross for us. Admit to Him that you are a sinner and cannot save yourself. Tell Him that you want the power to follow Him and trust Him for your life. Thank Him for dying in your place for us to receive eternal life through the grace He offers.

Only then will you find the riches in glory in Christ Jesus. To me, when we see Him face-to-face, that means finding out what we were actually created to be in His Kingdom. Imagine that! It can never be found in this life alone. We will learn it when we finally go to Him.

Those who die without Him will never have a chance to find this out, which is very sad. That is why I am, with many others, praying for a huge revival. I am hoping that through His story in my life, the nonbelieving reader will come to know Him personally. It will be the best decision anyone could ever make. Why? Salvation, the greatest miracle of all miracles, lasts forever.

Praise be to God for what Jesus did to earn it for us. It came at such a horrible price, but God the Son still went through with it because He loves us. What an incredible gift!

Please understand this, whatever God has created you to be will be more satisfying than anything this earth can offer. And that satisfaction will also last forever. I hope you will join all of us who have found His perfect peace offered in the Scriptures. His love endures forever, and with it His mercy, grace and peace. Once one has it, he will find there is nothing to compare to it.

There is one last thing I need to mention. There are people from different religious denominations and backgrounds that have confessed to me that they really don't know how to pray, let alone pray for salvation. Prayer is merely talking to and with God. But, as I mentioned, I had help from the Gideon Bible to make my prayer of salvation. Therefore, if you want to receive Jesus Christ as your personal Savior and Lord, pray something like this:

Lord Jesus, I am a sinner and cannot save myself. I have learned that Your Father sent You to die in my place on the cross to pay the full price of all my sins, past, present and future. I repent of my sin and want to receive you as my Savior and Lord. I want to follow You as You see fit. Please give me the faith to know what I have been missing. Please come into my heart as my one and only personal Savior and Lord. Thank You for the gift of eternal life with You. Thank You for loving me more than anyone on earth possibly could. And through that love, please make me the kind of person you want me to be. In Jesus precious name I pray, Amen.

If you just sincerely prayed this more modern form of the sinner's prayer, the Bible tells us that the angels are rejoicing in heaven. They are excited that you will be with God, all born-again believers, and the angels. It's a wonderful thought! One more relationship with Christ has been added to His church. Welcome to His Kingdom.

And all God's people said—**Amen!**

"For God so loved the world, that he gave his only son, that whoever believes in him shall not perish but have eternal life." (John 3:16 ESV)

Acknowledgments

I acknowledge the following people and groups:

My cousin Cris, author of *B Mom, Lovely Weeds*, did the major editing and made several suggestions. Cris helped me to realize that many nongolfers would not understand the terms used to explain the GHIO miracle. I began to look at other things in the book that needed more explanation with that attitude.

My first pastor and good friend, Ron Graff, for encouraging me to tell God's story of these miracles and for proofing my first manuscript. Ron not only wrote the foreword to the book but was very helpful with suggestions.

My first adult Sunday-school teacher, former pastor and good friend, Bruce Whittaker. Bruce was a huge help in understanding the doctrinal basis for my faith and much more, especially what Christian fellowship means.

My first Bible-study teacher, John Davis. Bruce and His wife Dorothy, my wife Donna, and I met with John and his wife Cheryl every Wednesday evening at their home for almost one full year. Others came also, but we were the regulars. John saw to it that we memorized the verses we would need for our spiritual growth. John provided the spiritual food, and his wife Cheryl provided great nutritious food.

My current pastor, Jim Remington, who has encouraged me in my teaching, and his wife, Claudia, who has been a blessing and encouragement to our entire church. Jim is an incredible pastor/teacher. He has a love for the Lord, His Word, and for our guests and members. He has an evangelist's heart for the lost and still gives an invitation every week, something which seems to have disappeared in many evangelic churches.

Our current adult Sunday school class, which I teach with two other men on a rotation basis. I love to teach the Word, especially to these friends. I've learned a lot from them. They have been very encouraging to us in our teaching. There is a lot of love for the Lord and each other in our class.

Dr. Bruce Bickel. His incredible Bible study in Pennsylvania was a real blessing to me. Over a three-year period, I felt I was attending the best seminary on earth.

Friends Bill Bingler, Jack Faulkner, and David Lipke. These old high school friends became believers and have really encouraged me in my teaching ministry and the writing of GHIO.

My sister Judy Starkey for helping me when it was definitely needed in my life, and my sister Janice Hays for being at the hospital when I needed her. Jan also encouraged me to write my book.

My three nieces, Julia, Janice, and Sarah, who kept me in stitches when they were young. They were fun to be around. I thank Janice Hilgencamp for giving me the book *Miracles* by Eric Metaxas. It was not only great information, but it kept me from duplicating a chapter or two.

My granddaughter Kate for teaching me to text and encouraging me to write GHIO. Kate is in college preparing to be a doctor.

My step-daughter Jennifer and her husband, my son-in-law Paul, and for our two wonderful grandchildren, Avery and Garrett, who have been such a blessing in my life. All have received Christ as their Savior and Lord. The grandkids, recent believers, are very excited about God.

My step daughter Michelle and her husband, Jay. Michelle has always been gracious to me since my first date with her mother.

My cousin Karen, an encouraging Christian friend and colleague who also teaches an adult Sunday school class. We call each other our crazy Christian cousins (CCC). She is CCC1 and I am CCC2. Karen's cousin Lou, a friend and fellow graduate from high school, I thank for introducing me to her. Karen was the first to preview the longer version of GHIO. I really appreciated her comments.

I am deeply grateful for these people for previewing *God's Hole-In-One and Other Miracles*: Pastor Ron Graff, Karen Wahab, David Gwyer, William Bingler, Jan Hilgencamp, Pastor Jim Remington, Tracee Swift, Bruce Whittaker, Joe Simmons, and Leslie Miller, who helped in additional editing for consistency, and especially, Penny Woods, who taught me many important lessons about content writing.

About the Author

John Corfield grew up in a little suburb outside of Pittsburgh along the Ohio River. His Presbyterian teaching about God meant a lot to him. While in a kindergarten Sunday-school class one day, as he was hanging up his coat, the thought that Jesus Christ is God somehow came to him. From that point on, he liked going to church. He tried to live the religious life he thought Jesus would want him to live. Lying, swearing, stealing, doing harm to others, or gossiping were things generally avoided because Jesus wouldn't like it. In fact, his friends began to call him "deacon."

He continued to live this way until the spring of eighth grade. One day, John did something he had never done; he took the Lord's name in vain. In his words, "My spiritual life went on a downhill slide after that." For many years, he became more and more involved with the world. God was not forgotten, just not as important any longer.

However, at the age of thirty-one, something changed his life. Through a series of miracles, John became a born-again Christian. One really bizarre miracle confirmed that his life would always be, in some way, a ministry to others.

Oddly enough, it happened one day on, of all places—**a golf course.**